Praise for *Animal Stars*

"*Animal Stars* is an inspiring tapestry, with emotions interwoven into every picture and word. We all know the feeling of connecting with our favorite animal — of their welcoming us, happier to see us than anyone else, and loving us unconditionally. This beautiful book is filled with stories of creatures great and small, all beloved companions and heroes, proving that the magic of life is indeed alive in the wondrous animals with whom we share this amazing planet. Let yourself soak in the love that flows from every page!"
— SIEGFRIED & ROY

"Each page of *Animal Stars* is star-studded, and I am thankful to say that what American Humane Association does can only be classified as 'a knockout.' So, yo, Rocky, knock yourself out and be sure to read *Animal Stars.*"
— CAROL CONNORS, two-time Academy Award–nominated songwriter and national spokesperson for AHA cat adoption

"If you are an animal lover and a fan of movies and television, this is a must-read. I found myself enthralled with the stories from filmmakers and trainers about how they achieved cinematic magic with these amazing animals!"
— CANDY SPELLING

"Through John Paul Pet we help care for, adopt, and save hundreds of thousands of our friends in the animal kingdom. All of them cannot say thank you with a smile, a wag of their tail, or a flip of their flipper, but the majority give us unconditional love. It's only honorable and fitting for people as special as Robin Ganzert and the Andersons to publish a book on how truly unique and special these animals are. This information is enjoyable and, most important, FUN!"
— JOHN PAUL DEJORIA, founder of John Paul Pet, cofounder and CEO of Paul Mitchell Hair Care, and cofounder and chairman of Patron Spirits

"A collaboration of animal lovers, protectors, and educators has conjured the perfect book for those who are inspired by the human-animal bond.

Thank you for taking us behind the scenes of the movie sets that have inspired us all." — PRINCE LORENZO BORGHESE, animal advocate

"Robin Ganzert and Allen and Linda Anderson give us a peek at what it takes to have Benji smile at just the right moment or let Hightower take Julia Roberts for the perfect ride. But these animals meant even more than that on the sets where they performed. Just as our companion animals do for us at home, these animal stars helped keep cast and crew grounded in reality, smiling whenever possible, and enjoying every day to the fullest. This is a great and enjoyable read."
— ROBERT VETERE, president and CEO, American Pet Products Association, and author of *From Wags to Riches*

"*Animal Stars* gets 5★s with a rating of G for 'great.' This is a book that needed to be written. As the principal veterinarian for most of the trainers interviewed in this book, I believe that it accurately portrays the bond that exists between animal trainers and their charges. For these trainers, working and communicating with animals is a calling — a lifetime commitment. Congratulations to American Humane Association for making this information available to the animal-loving public in such a highly readable format." — JAMES F. PEDDIE, DVM, veterinarian to many animal stars

ANIMAL
STARS

Also by Allen and Linda Anderson

Angel Animals: Divine Messengers of Miracles

Angel Animals Book of Inspiration:
Divine Messengers of Wisdom and Compassion

Angel Cats: Divine Messengers of Comfort

Angel Dogs: Divine Messengers of Love

Angel Dogs with a Mission: Divine Messengers in Service to All Life

Angel Horses: Divine Messengers of Hope

Animals and the Kids Who Love Them:
Extraordinary True Stories of Hope, Healing, and Compassion

A Dog Named Leaf: The Hero from Heaven Who Saved My Life

Dogs and the Women Who Love Them:
Extraordinary True Stories of Loyalty, Healing, and Inspiration

Horses with a Mission: Extraordinary True Stories of Equine Service

Rainbows and Bridges: An Animal Companion Memorial Kit

Rescued: Saving Animals from Disaster

Saying Goodbye to Your Angel Animals:
Finding Comfort after Losing Your Pet

ANIMAL STARS

Behind the Scenes with Your Favorite Animal Actors

Robin Ganzert, PhD
Allen & Linda Anderson

foreword by MARTY BECKER, DVM

New World Library
Novato, California

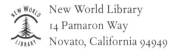

New World Library
14 Pamaron Way
Novato, California 94949

Text design by Tona Pearce Myers

Library of Congress Cataloging-in-Publication Data
Ganzert, Robin.
Animal stars : behind the scenes with your favorite animal actors / Robin Ganzert, PhD, and Allen and Linda Anderson ; foreword by Marty Becker, DVM.
     pages   cm
ISBN 978-1-60868-263-8 (hardback) — ISBN 978-1-60868-264-5 (ebook)
1. Animals on television. 2. Animals in motion pictures. I. Anderson, Allen, 1954–
II. Anderson, Linda C., 1946– III. Title.
PN1992.8.A58G36 2014
791.8—dc23   2014013765

First printing, September 2014
ISBN 978-1-60868-263-8
Printed in Canada on 100% postconsumer-waste recycled paper

New World Library is proud to be a Gold Certified Environmentally Responsible Publisher. Publisher certification awarded by Green Press Initiative. www.greenpressinitiative.org

10   9   8   7   6   5   4   3   2   1

CONTENTS

FOREWORD

Animals provide us with much joy and unconditional love, and I appreciate seeing them celebrated in entertainment. Animals in films remind us all of our own pets at home — and how much they improve our health and enrich our lives. This book shares inside stories about our favorite animal stars and the trainers and celebrities who work with them to create magical moments.

Animal actors often steal the show, and you just can't help but smile when they appear on-screen. I look back fondly on the animal stars of years past — from Benji to Black Beauty — and the happiness those beloved stars brought to so many. Today, animal stars like adventurous Crystal from *Night at the Museum* and adorable Uggie from *The Artist* seize the spotlight. This book features behind-the-scenes accounts of Benji, Crystal, and Uggie, as well as Finder's Key from *War Horse*, Hightower from *The Horse Whisperer*, Casey the bear from the *Jungle Book* movies, and Crackerjack from the Harry Potter films, to name only a few of the animals who have stolen hearts around the world and whom you'll meet in the following pages.

American Humane
Association board member
Marty Becker, DVM,
"America's Veterinarian"

This book also showcases the animal trainers who bring incredible scenes to life for the camera. Their patience, devotion, and carefulness will renew for you the life-affirming power of the human-animal bond. Their insightful training tips will make the time you spend with your own pets more enjoyable and safer.

These stories charmed me, just as animal stars have done for years in my favorite movies. In the almost twenty years I've spent working in network television, where I've talked about animal health on programs such as *Good Morning America* and *The Dr. Oz Show*, I have shared how to improve the lives of both pets and people. Now you will get a peek into the lives of animal stars — and how they became world-famous icons who linger in our imaginations and hearts long after their images have faded from movie and TV screens.

On behalf of the animals in film and entertainment, I am grateful to American Humane Association (AHA). I serve on the board of directors for AHA and know well their efforts to protect these animals. For over seventy years, AHA's Film and Television Unit has demonstrated an unsurpassed commitment to ensuring the humane treatment of animal actors. Here's a round of "a-paws" for their efforts.

As you discover the backgrounds, training, and versatility of animal stars through the stories in this book, it may surprise you to learn that many of them were rescue animals, rejected by people who had no idea what treasures they were giving away. Their losses, our gains. From homelessness, these animals went on to lead fulfilling lives as actors and, in their time off, as family pets. Many of the compelling stories of these multi-talented film and television animals and their successful trainers / best friends are revealed for the first time in these pages.

> **DID YOU KNOW...?**
>
> In 1881, Eadweard Muybridge showed the first sequential photographs of animal locomotion, which included a trotting horse. This is considered the birth of film. And an animal led the way.

As a veterinarian, I found this book reassuring. As a movie buff and animal lover, I found it delightful, honest, informative, and immensely entertaining.

Now, on with the show!

— Marty Becker, DVM, nationally syndicated columnist,
chief veterinary correspondent for *The Dr. Oz Show*,
and author of twenty-two books

ACTION!

I thought the centaur was a mythological creature
until I watched Bobby Lovgren and Finder interacting.
At one point, I could not tell man from horse.
They both performed admirably.

– Steven Spielberg, director, *War Horse*

*T*he director calls, *"Action!"* The set slips into silence. A tiny Chihuahua
sprints to the stage without prompting and positions herself on a
mark. Her bright eyes focus on the camera with its blinking light. She's
ready for her close-up.

Temperature is their friend and foe. Penguins waddle around the
soundstage, heading for the fish bucket, while human actors and a movie
crew shiver in the cold that these marine mammals require. If a car commercial's director truly believes it won't hurt a Siberian lynx to sit on hot-
midday-sun pavement, a feisty trainer advises him to pull *his* pants down
and let his backside touch the desert road.

Expectations must be met. Wolves, raised by hand from pups, are
taught to snarl on cue and anticipate a reward. They'd rather lick their
trainer's face than actually get mad at anyone. Crew members on location
for a film shoot drive eighty miles to the nearest KFC to bring back the
Original Recipe chicken a massive black bear expects for his treats.

Pride and consciousness make them individuals. A Thoroughbred im-
presses a world-renowned director with his athletic prowess but finds it
unbearably boring to stand still while actors repeat lines of dialogue. A

blue conure brilliantly learns over a hundred new tricks, even adding his own variations, and carries the fate of a movie on his wings.

Animals rescued from shelters excel at the work. Seal point Himalayan cats, found through animal rescue organizations, play a dysfunctional family's feline in a hit movie series. In an iconic scene, one of the cats attempts to flush the family's dog down the toilet and becomes the subject of national news articles. A shelter dog spends three days of quality time with his human costar. Then he expertly performs in nearly every scene of an Academy Award–winning movie and encourages people to adopt older shelter dogs.

These adored animals perform for food, praise, toys, and attention. They jump into vans, take naps in kennels, and pace themselves through days and nights on the job. Their acute sense of smell makes them easily distracted by aromas wafting from craft service vans providing meals for the cast and crew. Sometimes, they're focused on the task at hand; other times, they just want to play.

Their photos in news stories bring smiles to moviegoers' and animal lovers' faces. They stir frenzies over their breeds and are ambassadors for entire species. Their images fill big and small screens with presence, personality, intelligence, sincerity, and love. They delight children and adults. They move audiences to tears yet often mystify people who work with them. They have fan clubs and Facebook pages. They need safe passage through their days on earth and are remembered long after all-too-short lives.

Their voices can be heard as raucous barks, friendly nickers, soothing purrs, and cheerful chirps, although humans must speak up for them. Their soulful eyes reflect whatever purity and innocence dwell in the interior life of our species. The world is a better place because they appeal to and draw out our highest natures, our best selves.

They are animal stars.

Learning the Secrets and Discovering Training Tips

We've all been moved by animal stars during their performances, but what we discovered was that there are even more amazing and inspiring

Robin Ganzert and
Crystal on a film set

stories behind the scenes. In the chapters that follow, respected trainers, actors, directors, and animal advocates reveal what happens offscreen and behind the scenes with the animals who light up movie, television, and computer screens. In addition, certified animal safety representatives from American Humane Association (AHA) share fascinating details about the work they do while monitoring animals on film sets.

When Robin Ganzert visited a set and met trainer Thomas Gunderson and the capuchin Crystal from the *Night at the Museum* movies, the little monkey gave her a unique shampoo and hairstyle. Crystal jumped from trainer Tom's arms onto Robin's shoulder and slathered her hair with flavored yogurt.

To accurately research and thoroughly write this book, we interviewed each of the trainers who have stories and photos in it. In some cases, we visited homes and facilities where working and retired animal actors live. We met, petted, and played with animal icons of the silver screen. We were gratified to witness firsthand the love and devotion these trainers show for the animals in their care. Animals returned their trainers' love in unmistakable ways with tail wagging, licking, and body language that says, "I'm happy and excited to see you again."

Finder (from *War Horse*) with Linda and Allen Anderson at Bobby Lovgren's ranch

We have organized the stories in this book into four parts. Though part 3 is devoted exclusively to dogs and their trainers, some of the trainers in part 2 have stories about various animals they train, including dogs.

In addition to the stories they contributed, we asked this book's exemplary trainers to provide some "secret sauce" for readers who want tips for training and handling their own pets. They generously offered practical animal-training advice at the end of their stories. The trainers also share information about where beloved animal stars came from, what might be in their future, who loves and cares for them, and how they do the remarkable things that amaze and endear them to audiences worldwide.

The Role of Animal Stars

Animal actors remind people of the importance of touch and physical, emotional, and spiritual connection.

If an animal appears to get hurt on-screen, it breaks our hearts. When animals look as if they're having fun and make us laugh, our stress levels plummet. We're all glad when special effects prevent anyone from taking risks with the health and safety of animal actors. However, most people we spoke with about animals in filmed entertainment agreed that although computer-generated imagery (CGI) and animal animatronics (puppetlike machines that imitate animals) can enhance the portrayal of animals, nothing compares to having a camera focus on a real animal's soulful eyes and genuine body language.

DID YOU KNOW...?

American Humane Association was founded in 1877 to advocate on behalf of children and animals. View a video clip narrated by Shirley MacLaine by going to www.youtube.com/user/american humane and clicking on "AHA Tribute Piece" or by scanning the QR code below.

In this era and culture, human entertainers often share way too much information with their adoring fans. It's only fair that some public spotlight now shines on the horses these actors literally rode in on or the dogs who trotted beside them or the movie cats who slept on their beds. It's long overdue that the moviegoing public comes to know and appreciate animal actors — their histories and the trainers who work and live with them.

The roles that animal actors play evoke emotion, inspire compassion, and create impressions that no other creature or technology can. Animals are at the heart and soul of every movie or show in which they appear.

Part 1

HORSE STARS
AND THEIR TRAINERS

Finder jumping and playing on the set of *War Horse*

While the rest of us remember the names of celebrities in our favorite movies, Beth Langhorst tends to recall actors with names like Pumpkin, Thunder, Cimarron, and Crackerjack. Her focus is strictly on animal safety. She backs up her recommendations and decisions with hard facts and science. She takes pride in having made a difference for animals over the years. Risking animal safety and health in the entertainment industry is simply not open for discussion.

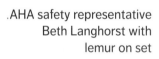
.AHA safety representative Beth Langhorst with lemur on set

As a senior certified animal safety representative, resource coordinator, and set support representative, Beth has worked at American Humane Association (AHA) since 1998. She graduated from the Moorpark College Exotic Animal Training and Management Program and worked as a zookeeper in the education department of the San Diego Zoo. Then she was a trainer on set for an animal company. She has worked on countless movies, television shows, and commercials and was the AHA safety representative for all four *Pirates of the Caribbean* films.

Africa and Horses

Over the years, Beth has done a number of international jobs as an AHA safety representative. In Africa, she's had to explain that even though animals' work is to help herders provide for their families — they're not treated as family members — the camels must have shade. "I had a lot of battles on the African shoot when I was there for three months," Beth recalls. "The horse wranglers asked why they couldn't use a BB gun and shoot the horse to make him run. An Australian wrangler got so angry that he shot *me* with his BB gun."

In her job, Beth must communicate with the local people to help her research the terrain that horses and other animals will have to negotiate. Movie settings are originally chosen for their beauty or utility, not with animal safety in mind. There could be logs, fallen trees, and branches hidden under deep snow that might cause a horse to trip. Pointy rocks may protrude from the ground with even more rocks underneath, making hazardous conditions for any horse, but especially for those who are used to running through rolling grassy fields. "Most of the time, the director and producer will see the danger I'm pointing out," Beth says. "They don't want to do the scene in a way or at a place where animals could be harmed."

In one shoot that Beth was on in Africa, the horses were required to run up and down a steep hill composed of grainy sand with rocks in it. The director wanted to use that specific hill, which even had its own name, because the only other possible hill for use was over an hour's drive away. Besides, it was too late in the shoot to change locations. "Every horse for this scene was local, in tip-top shape, and ridden by a proficient rider," Beth explains. "The horses were used to the humidity, heat, and terrain, yet finding their footing and staying on the path would be difficult." Beth was pleased that the wranglers let the horses

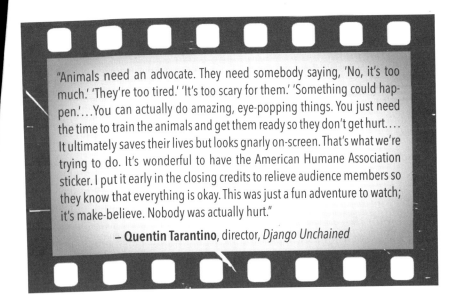

"Animals need an advocate. They need somebody saying, 'No, it's too much.' 'They're too tired.' 'It's too scary for them.' 'Something could happen.'....You can actually do amazing, eye-popping things. You just need the time to train the animals and get them ready so they don't get hurt.... It ultimately saves their lives but looks gnarly on-screen. That's what we're trying to do. It's wonderful to have the American Humane Association sticker. I put it early in the closing credits to relieve audience members so they know that everything is okay. This was just a fun adventure to watch; it's make-believe. Nobody was actually hurt."

— **Quentin Tarantino**, director, *Django Unchained*

Since then, AHA has protected animal actors for over seventy years. It is the only organization officially sanctioned by the film and television industry to do this work for animals around the globe. The AHA staff has special expertise that allows them to be a voice on behalf of animal actors. Their track record says it all: AHA's Film and Television Unit has a 99.98 percent safety record for animals on the sets of filmed media.

Remarkable Horses and Trainers

In the next section of this book, you'll meet remarkable horses who star in films. They amaze with their intelligence, talent, and intuition. There are risks involved with filming horses, whose legs and joints are delicate, whose temperaments affect their performance, and whose fight-or-flight natures can cause them to stampede. The following stories show the meticulous care that is taken of horses like Finder, who played Joey in Steven Spielberg's *War Horse*; Hightower, the horse Julia Roberts rode in *Runaway Bride*; and Cimarron, who swam with Hailee Steinfeld across a raging river in *True Grit*.

instinctively make their way down the hill. The scene succeeded accidents.

What's Important?

Beth looks back in wonder on her many experiences of keeping ani safe under the most difficult conditions. As much as she loves anin and cares deeply about them, she has to stay completely professional a focused in the present to make these projects safe for the horses.

Each movie Beth works on gets its shots planned with as much atten tion to detail, communication, and teamwork as possible. Beth says, "You can train animals. You can get things that look insanely crazy and dangerous done safely. You just have to take the time to do it. At the end of the day, even though there is a lot to take into consideration for a movie, and the trainers and I work together, I am responsible for the safety of these animals."

Beth and the other AHA safety representatives work cooperatively with but independently of producers, directors, movie and television studios, actors, crew members, and animal trainers. They aren't interested in whether a filmed project is funny, sad, or scary. It doesn't matter if the movie is creative, profitable, or filled with glitzy stars. They draw on a long history of protecting animals in filmed media.

After the 1939 movie *Jesse James*, AHA opened its western regional office in Hollywood, California, to fight cruelty to animals in film and television. During the filming of *Jesse James*, in a horrific act of blatant disregard for animal safety, a terrified, blindfolded horse was forced to carry a cowboy while jumping off a cliff into a lake. The cowboy lived. The defenseless horse broke his back and died.

In 1940, AHA picketed the movie industry for using wires to trip horses so they would fall for the camera. The Motion Picture Production Code (known as the Hays Code at the time) condemned the practice of horse tripping. AHA and the Motion Picture Producers and Distributors of America (which became the Motion Picture Association of America) stated that AHA safety representatives should be consulted on all films requiring animals and be on set to supervise animal action.

Chapter 1

BOBBY LOVGREN

(SOUTHERN CALIFORNIA)

and STEVEN SPIELBERG

Director Steven Spielberg (right) observes Jeremy Irvine (left) rehearse a scene with Joey (Finder) on the set of DreamWorks Pictures' *War Horse*, an epic adventure set against a sweeping canvas of rural England and continental Europe during World War I

Finder as Joey in *War Horse*
A Director's Dream Actor

Bobby Lovgren

Imagine you are sitting in on the following fictional scene of a film-school class where a famous director is guest lecturer. A student with a short beard and intense eyes raises his hand. "How would you describe the best actor you ever directed? What makes this actor so great?"

The student lowers his hand. A hush descends on the room. The class and its instructor wait, fingers hovering over laptops, ready to take notes. The director takes a moment before answering.

"If I were to describe my ideal actor, I'd say, 'He's so natural on film that you would never know he's a professional actor. No matter what goes on around him, he stays focused. He doesn't complain about shooting scenes over and over and from different angles. He's an individual with a unique personality and attitude, a bit of a ham, actually. Not a little soldier doing what he's told, but an actor who always brings something special to the scene. My job is to help his natural talents shine. When the cameras roll, he gives 100 percent to the performance. He's prepared and energetic and enjoys his work.'"

The students applaud. The instructor, arms folded across his chest, stands in the back of the room. He calls out, "Have you ever worked with an actor like that?" Our imaginary director in this college classroom smiles slyly. "Yes, I have," he says. "My best Hollywood actor is named Finder's Key. Finder, for short." The director makes a dramatic pause. "And he's a horse."

My Ideal Equine Actor

The director in the made-up scene above, when describing his ideal actor, has listed the qualities of Finder, my multitalented, fourteen-year-old gelding. Finder is best known for his outstanding role as Joey in the

2011 Steven Spielberg–directed, Oscar-nominated film *War Horse*, the World War I story of Albert Narracott, played by Jeremy Irvine. Albert is a young man who follows his horse, Joey, into war, determined to be reunited with him. I was the horse master, as the position is called in England, and head trainer / head wrangler on the movie, in charge of managing 150 horses, horse handlers, trainers, and groomers, who did fantastic work.

Ten Andalusians and Warmbloods from Europe and Hungary played Joey from foal to adulthood. Finder played Joey in key scenes: breaking away from the military officers after Joey was sold; Joey jumping over a tank; and Joey being trapped by fake barbed wire in the pivotal no-man's-land scene. Finder also took on the role of Joey's mother when Joey was a foal. My Finder stayed with me after the filming was completed, and all the other horses also went to good homes.

Finder is not a horse actor who does scenes in which a human actor rides him. His talent is specialty work. He performs specific actions "loose," or at liberty. Because of his unique talents, we flew him to the *War Horse* set in England, from his home at my ranch in Southern California. Finder has a presence about him that I've never found in any other horse. I'm fortunate to have harnessed his boundless energy and channeled it in a positive direction into his movie roles. We succeed in large part because Finder and I have a relationship built on mutual trust and respect.

Finding Finder

I was a trainer on *Seabiscuit* when I met Finder's Key, one of two horses doing specialty scenes. A typical Thoroughbred, full of energy, he played the part of a racehorse. In *Seabiscuit*, he hadn't run in racing scenes but was in segments in which a jockey would be holding on to him. He was never at liberty. I bought him after the filming finished, not thinking he would become such an excellent equine actor. I just liked his personality and style.

I went to Africa for about a year to train horses and zebras for the movie *Racing Stripes*. Finder stayed at the ranch, which meant I didn't get to work with him. Then we got a job on *The Legend of Zorro*, and I was able to start seeing what he could do. I had to work with his high energy and help him learn to focus it. He clearly showed potential as an excellent scene-stealer.

By the time we had been together for two years, Finder's unique qualities had begun to emerge. During the time away from me, he had matured. He was chosen for the lead role in *Wildfire*, a racehorse television series. Every week, different episodes required him to learn new skills. That's when I discovered how much he enjoyed working. As I got to know what he was good at, I asked him to do those things.

Becoming an Equine Actor Trainer

Many of the techniques I initially learned for the work of training equine actors came from exposure to skilled trainers as a child and, later, as an adult. My parents owned one of the largest jumping and dressage barns in South Africa, so I grew up in the horse business. I worked as a stable manager at Brentwood Park Stables for five years, the largest eventing and jumping stable in South Africa. Some American trainers came to our place, where we did films and commercials, and I became interested in having a career like theirs.

Twenty-two years ago, I moved to the United States and met Glenn Randall Sr., who trained horses for *Ben-Hur* and *The Roy Rogers Show*. He and his son Corky Randall, who worked on all of the Black Stallion films, helped me get into the equine actor business and taught me the basics of training horses for film work. Glenn and Corky Randall originated modern-day practices of horse trainers and wranglers for movies — everything from safety to procedures and philosophy. From those beginnings with the Randalls, I progressed and learned on my own. My first big film was *The Mask of Zorro* with Antonio Banderas, for which I was a horse trainer.

The most important thing I've learned is to be very, very patient. There's a big difference between being a regular horse trainer working with animals at home and having an animal trained for film. On a movie set, the trainer has to know how the camera works and what is required for filmmaking. There can be as many as two hundred people milling around doing their jobs. The horse must be able to do whatever he needs in order to work at liberty, in the midst of all those people and distractions. In *War Horse*, the horses also dealt with smoke, loud noises, and dust while working with special effects to stage the scenes.

A technique I've used for a long time, which I learned from the Randalls, is not to confuse the animal with changes. A horse will have confidence in a trainer if he's consistent. Sometimes, trainers feel pressure to teach horses behaviors within short time frames. But our schedules make no difference to the animals. Successful training requires having the patience to make sure the horse understands exactly what is supposed to be achieved. The simpler I keep the training for a horse, the easier it is for him to learn.

Some animals work for food, but I've found that the biggest reward for an equine actor, after he's done a job well, is to leave him alone. I've observed animals in nature and noticed that when a mare gives her foal milk and she thinks the baby has had enough, she'll push him away. So when a horse does a behavior properly, I pet him and go away.

If the horse works for food, when he isn't hungry, he stops working. It's difficult for me when people on film sets carry apples around from craft (food) services or an actor shows up for the scene with an apple or carrots in his hand. I like to keep things simple. Do your job, and your reward is to be left alone so you can rest or play. That works with a horse's nature much better than giving him treats at night at the barn door or feeding him by hand after he's finished a task.

Finder's Unique Talents

Understanding your animal is critical because the trainer must tune in to what the animals are thinking. How aware of the task at hand is the animal? Is he paying attention to you? For a film, the horse may need to do the same thing in the same place ten or fifteen times in a row, to the point that it becomes monotonous. For some animals, the repetition is difficult or boring, and they refuse to do it anymore. Not Finder.

Finder is the most challenging animal I've worked with because he loves when cameras and people are around. They energize him. A professional, he brings something new to each scene. Like anyone who takes pride in his work, if he does something wrong and I raise my voice to him, he pouts. That's the best word I can use to describe the look he gets on his face. I've never seen it in another animal.

Finder enjoys his work and doesn't like being left out. If he's not the main focus in a movie, I play with him and let him relax, which makes the day better for both of us. But he wants to work. If I walk past his stall, he watches to see if I'm coming to get him for a scene or rehearsal. The other horses will continue eating, but Finder is always the first one to want to go anywhere.

I bring him with me to my jobs whether he's in the movie or not. He thrives on a film set. I also make sure he has time off to just be a horse, to play and rest. This keeps our work and relationship fresh and fun. When he is not on a job, he only exercises to stay fit. This gives him a break from having me tell him what to do.

When Finder isn't filming, he might be staying at a horse trailer on set (*War Horse* had temporary stables on-site for the horses), eating and drinking, or resting. Equine actors must learn to be comfortable in different environments. Filming goes on morning, afternoon, and evening, so the horses have to relax in between tasks and conserve their energy. We use doubles, with nontoxic paint on them to create identical spots. That way, no one horse ever gets too tired, which could make them prone to mistakes or injury.

Finder and Houdini

At home, Finder was attached to an older horse named Houdini who lived next to him in the stable. When someone took Houdini away, Finder nickered and acted lonely. Houdini was his best horse friend. But Houdini was kind of bossy, and he ruled the pasture and stable. He nipped at Finder when it was time for their dinner. As long as there was no food involved, Houdini and Finder could be friends.

Houdini and Finder were a great team working together. Houdini was a behind-the-scenes kind of hero, while his more flamboyant counterpart got all the credit. Houdini did 90 percent of the work, and Finder did the exceptional acting. Houdini was always there to back up Finder and gave us confidence we would succeed. He could do everything Finder did but was quiet about his accomplishments. His work at liberty was amazing. Yet he was gentle enough that anyone could ride him, including the actors. He even taught my children to ride.

Houdini passed away on my birthday in 2013. In less than two hours, he got colic, and because he was suffering and couldn't recover, we had to put him down at the age of twenty-two. We were all home, except for my youngest child, and said good-bye to him. Houdini was so much a part of our family. His passing was hard on all of us. I am grateful that he had such an exceptional life.

Horses as Actors

As with noticing and building on Houdini's quiet competence, one of my biggest jobs is to recognize each horse's strengths, enhance those skills, and not ask them to do something they aren't good at or don't enjoy doing. I can tell within the first fifteen minutes whether Finder will be able to do a task. I don't push him, because I know his limitations. This is another reason why we use multiple horses to play a role. If the horse is happy doing what is required for the scene, he's much better at it.

Finder is probably one of the most famous, talked-about horses ever. He is unbelievable. He runs and is playful. As long as he is moving and jumping, he is fine. Being still for a long period of time is as tough for Finder as asking my energetic son to settle down. Finder is not a patient, quiet horse. He can't tolerate and isn't capable of doing nothing in a scene that is shot for an hour so the actor can repeat dialogue. A shoot like that is torturous for him. Don't ask him. He'll fight it. Standing still is not his job.

I help bring out Finder's personality and reactions for the camera. Although some might not call what he does acting, I've noticed that he heightens his actions when people are around. He lets me create emotions for him to show, and the expressions on his face make him easy to read. I've never seen a more expressive horse. He's essentially happy, but when the role requires it, he acts wild in a controlled way.

Finder's trust in me is absolute. When we filmed the *War Horse* scene in which it looked as if he was trapped in no-man's-land, he had to convey a lot of emotion, show the whites of his eyes, and roll his eyes back in his head as if he was afraid. Although he wasn't actually in any distress, the scene took place in mud, water, and rain, which none of us liked. We needed to have confidence in each other to make it look as if he was in danger.

For actors to feel comfortable and natural while filming with horses, they need to spend a lot of time with the animals prior to filming. In *War Horse*, actor Jeremy Irvine got to know the horses by helping with grooming and cleaning their stalls.

But typically, Finder doesn't care if the actor is in a scene with him or not. While the actor is doing actions and saying dialogue, it only appears as if the horse is relating to him. I stay within eyesight of and have control over the horse, who is actually listening to me, not the actor.

Safety First and Foremost

I never take a risk with my equine actors. This is why I spend so much time preparing for a film and rehearsing sequences. I am a small piece in the jigsaw puzzle of movie making, and I must communicate well. Trainers without enough professional experience or education tend not to be as good at communicating with directors, and that can lead to more mistakes.

It is difficult when the director wants the horse to do something and I have to say he can't perform that action safely. I discuss complex shots with the director months ahead of time. I offer several options for how to achieve something for the camera, explain what horses can do, and show that the director's vision will still be fulfilled. In *War Horse*, computer-generated imagery (CGI) special effects and an animatronic horse performed tasks that real horses couldn't do. No matter how dangerous a scene looks on film, I've spent many hours preparing to do it without risk to the horse.

The WWII tank that Joey leaped over in *War Horse* could not have fit into a good-sized living room. We had to build a ramp for Finder to run up and jump across the tank during the scene when the tank was supposed to block Joey from following Albert. Finder jumped three feet and kept going after reaching the other side of the tank. We shot it at an old airfield they built the set on. When I went to the site, it was so realistic that I felt as if I was entering a war zone. I would not want to go there by myself; it was that real. We did several small takes without any CGI. It ended up being a goose bumps kind of scene.

Finder and Bobby Lovgren

A disappointment to me is that because so much is done with CGI, moviegoers and reviewers assume the horse action that we have so carefully and safely produced isn't real. For the movie *Racing Stripes*, filmed in South Africa, I trained a horse and a zebra who had to work at liberty together. Some people who saw the movie thought that 90 percent of the horse-and-zebra action was CGI and 10 percent was real, but it was actually the other way around.

War Horse received the highest animal safety certification rating awarded by American Humane Association (AHA). A veterinarian was also on set daily. I find the AHA representatives are also helpful when

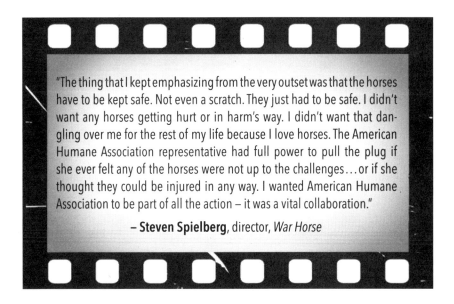

"The thing that I kept emphasizing from the very outset was that the horses have to be kept safe. Not even a scratch. They just had to be safe. I didn't want any horses getting hurt or in harm's way. I didn't want that dangling over me for the rest of my life because I love horses. The American Humane Association representative had full power to pull the plug if she ever felt any of the horses were not up to the challenges … or if she thought they could be injured in any way. I wanted American Humane Association to be part of all the action – it was a vital collaboration."

– Steven Spielberg, director, *War Horse*

people, such as extras or someone from the public, have a concern. I don't have time to explain something like "Yes, I have a whip in my hand, but I'm not using it on the horse. If he was scared of me, he'd be running away. It is simply an extension of my arm to direct him." The AHA representative will talk to the person and reassure him that the animal is not being mistreated.

Finder's Future

Because I travel so much and it's not cost-effective to buy every horse I train, I only personally own three horses. Finder is one of them, and I keep him with me wherever I go. Every time we work together, he surprises me with how much he enjoys the job. I'm astounded that he does not act like any horse I've ever been around. He's the best and the most difficult for me to work with. I must treat him differently than any other horse because of his strong personality and high intelligence.

Finder doesn't walk onto a scene; he swaggers. That's what makes him so eye appealing. He has attitude. I am so grateful for my relationship with him. I don't usually know what is next in our film future. But

Finder is a wonderful equine actor, and I know our friendship will continue forever.

Tips for Training Horses from Bobby Lovgren

Horses don't care what the movie is about or how much pressure you are under to have them quickly learn a behavior or action. Often, horse trainers are under pressure from the studios to get the horse to do something fast. They tell us to send them a video so they can make decisions. I can't let those requests influence what I do with horses. Patience is the most important quality to have when training any animal.

Another factor in training animals is that the animal might not have the ability to do what you are asking. Then you have to question whether you are asking too much. Is this horse athletic? Docile? Skittish? After you figure out the skill level and personality, you can treat a horse on his level, not yours.

I get much more success if I break down actions into small parts in a logical progression and know exactly what I am trying to teach the horse. If you have brought the action down to the horse's level and he has the aptitude for what you want him to do, you have a chance of teaching it to him.

Sometimes, people want to make a horse into a dog or some sort of domesticated pet. They go against the animal's nature. You cannot make a horse into a human and treat him as you would people or house pets. Treat him as a horse, and you'll have a better relationship with him.

Bobby Lovgren and Finder

Steven Spielberg

I thought the centaur was a mythological creature until I watched Bobby Lovgren and Finder interacting. At one point, I could not tell man from horse. They both performed admirably.

I gave Bobby a wish list of the moments I was hoping a horse could achieve. I am not a horse whisperer, so I directed Bobby to direct Finder. Bobby was always very honest with me when he thought what I was asking would not be possible. But there were very few things I asked that Bobby said, "That's not practical."

Almost everything I was hoping for could be achieved through Bobby. Bobby and Finder achieved beyond my wildest dreams.

Working with Finder and Bobby and American Humane Association [AHA] was a great experience. In areas of animal safety, I always deferred to Bobby and Barbara Carr, the AHA safety representative. Before the start of filming, I told both Bobby and Barbara that if they ever perceived anything that could put any of these horses in jeopardy, I would cancel the shot and rewrite the sequence with the safety of the animals first and foremost in my heart.

Chapter 2

CARI SWANSON
with REX PETERSON
(AMENIA, NEW YORK)
and JULIA ROBERTS

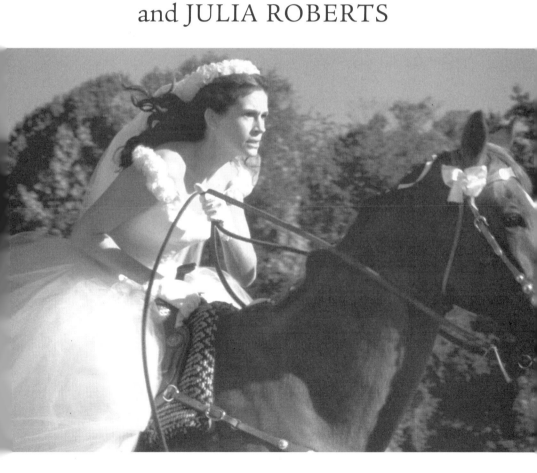

Julia Roberts and Hightower in *Runaway Bride*

Hightower in *The Horse Whisperer* and *Runaway Bride*

The Horse with an Actors' Equity Card

Cari Swanson with Rex Peterson

I was working on a photography project when I met legendary horse trainer and master horseman Rex Peterson. I tracked him down at his ranch in California after watching the movie *Hidalgo*. I wanted to meet and photograph RJ Masterbug (RJ), one of the horses Rex trained to play Hidalgo in the movie. Rex and I became friends and spoke often about training difficult horses. After a couple of years, I talked him into selling RJ to me. Rex cautioned me that, as a trick horse, RJ might have "too many buttons" that could cause trouble if I wasn't careful.

Rex came to my farm in New York to teach clinics and continued training RJ. Soon, I was working with RJ on film and television productions. Now, Rex and I are friends and business partners. We travel around the country teaching clinics and developing DVDs and products to help people train their horses.

Rex grew up in Ogallala, Nebraska, with seven siblings who all did trick riding in their youth. At seventeen, he traveled with his family to Japan to ride in a Wild West show for five weeks. Rex went on to learn the skill and craft of training movie horses from his mentor, master Hollywood trainer Glenn Randall Sr. (Glenn trained the Triggers for Roy Rogers, horses for *Ben-Hur*, and the last horse Gene Autry rode on-screen.)

Although Rex trained many outstanding horses, Hightower was the one who won his heart. A sixteen-hand, sorrel Thoroughbred, Hightower had excellent "frog eye" — wide, large, round eyes strategically situated on the skull that allow for exceptional peripheral vision. He had a short, beautiful, well-muscled, arched neck and outstanding balance and self-confidence, which Rex attributed to thousands of hours of correct training.

Cari Swanson and
RJ Masterbug

A gelding from Beaumont, California, Hightower was two years old when he was given to Rex in 1984. For five years, Hightower worked as Rex's horse while Rex lassoed and roped bulls at his California ranch in the mountains. It takes a certain personality and character for a horse to face the enormous, aggressive bulls. Rex grew to admire Hightower's strength and determination and his ability to calmly handle challenging work.

In 1989, Rex took three horses to work on the movie *Winter People*. In one scene, the horse needed to drag a dummy a long distance. When none of the three horses had the stamina to do the job for repeated takes, Rex brought in Hightower for his first movie appearance. He says, "Hightower dragged the dummy with the same determination he used on the ranch. When he showed his strength take after take, I knew he had the makings of a great movie horse."

Hightower's Movie Talents

Hightower and Rex formed a team that resulted in memorable and spectacular movies and scenes. Because Rex cross-trains his horses, Hightower became proficient in more than one area of education and proved to be a stellar athlete and performer. He could be ridden Western, English, and driven styles and was so well trained at liberty that during his career, he remained unmatched. He performed in scenes in which he herded calves while the cowboys who rode him roped wild bulls and trained mules. He jumped five feet effortlessly and even competed in dressage. He could drive single-, double-, and multihorse hitches.

Rex calls Hightower a "workaholic" who showed up to work and did his job seriously, giving his all every time. "Anyone could ride him," Rex says. "But I could call him out from under any rider." The rider might be moving away with Hightower, but if Rex whistled, Hightower would turn and run toward Rex. He taught Hightower many cues and could direct the horse to travel, spin, or turn, regardless of what the rider in the saddle was asking Hightower to do. "Hightower always listened to me, no matter what," Rex recalls. "We had tremendous respect and faith in one another. He had the desire to do anything I asked of him."

Rex remembers Hightower as honest, with a big heart. "When the going got tough, Hightower just got better." Rex could show the horse something once, and Hightower would understand it immediately. He rarely became confused or misunderstood what Rex needed him to do.

One scene required Hightower to drag a two-hundred-pound dummy from three-quarters of a mile away. He had to come from out of sight (called a "can't see") to run out of sight on the other end (called a "can't see in"). Rex set two radios a distance away from each other in the field. One radio was set to channel one and the other was on channel two. Rex first called Hightower from channel one. Another person, working as the horse's spotter, told Rex when Hightower got close to the first radio. Then Rex switched to channel two and called the horse to the second radio. Hightower flawlessly ran to Rex's voice both times and found him down in a gully out of camera range.

With Rex as head trainer for the movie, Hightower won the starring role of Pilgrim in *The Horse Whisperer* after impressing Robert Redford by charging on command. While filming the movie, Rex asked Hightower to do multiple tasks. Most horses would have tired and quit after a few attempts at the tasks. But long days at work didn't deter Hightower from giving his all every time. The horse was professional for every take.

Hightower knew when he was on camera and acted differently than when in rehearsals. His demeanor was laid-back for the walk-throughs of a scene. But when he heard the call "Rolling!" for the camera to start filming, he lit up and gave a stellar performance every time. In Hightower's later years as a movie horse, he would step out of his trailer, looking stiff, and then stretch like a cat. But as soon as he knew the camera was rolling, he moved with the grace and fluidity of a youngster.

Rex called Hightower "a horse with a heart as big as the outdoors" who was serious about every task and immensely versatile. He became an all-time-great Hollywood equine star. He even had his own Actors' Equity card. "Hightower always had faith and worked to please me," Rex says. "He responded to my praising him with my voice and patting him on his neck. He gloated when he did something right and looked to me for affirmation. He knew numerous voice commands and could tell what I wanted by my intonation and voice. We read each other's moods and worked accordingly."

Hightower Recruited for *Runaway Bride*

The production manager for *Runaway Bride* had seen what Hightower could do in *The Horse Whisperer* and requested him for her film. Julia Roberts developed a special bond with Hightower. After Julia rode Hightower in the initial shots for the film, he went to California to work on another project. Garry Marshall, the director, added new scenes to *Runaway Bride*. Julia requested that Hightower return to the set in Baltimore so she could ride him in the scenes. *Runaway Bride* needed him on a Monday, and he was supposed to work on his new project on the previous Friday. The only way to get Hightower to *Runaway Bride* over the weekend was to send him by FedEx plane early Saturday morning and drive him from JFK Airport for a Monday morning call on set.

Rex's Commitment to Safety

Rex says that Hightower "did not have an ounce of wanting to hurt anyone." To protect the horse, Rex prepared each shot carefully. In *The Horse Whisperer*, for example, the opening sequence has a truck coming around a bend while driving on a sheet of ice. It had to slide and appear to hit the horses, Pilgrim (Hightower) and Gulliver. The truck needed to stop at a specific spot so the horses would not actually be hit. Rex and the stunt coordinator, who also understood the need for keeping the horses safe, cabled off the area. The truck could not drive beyond a certain point under any circumstances and would only look as if it was hitting the horses. Rex says, "I will not risk the safety of my horses or cast and crew by going cheap. Even when studios want to cut costs, I will only work under safe circumstances and take the time to prepare the horses for a successful shot."

One of the movies Rex is most proud of is *Hidalgo*. Its challenges included logistical and communications breakdowns, working with powerful stud horses and difficult cast members, and country, cultural, and language barriers. The film was shot in numerous locations in Morocco, Montana, and California. But Rex is known for saving productions thousands of dollars and hours of work because of his ability to break down the sequence of tasks his horses must do and prepare and deliver what is required.

> **DID YOU KNOW...?**
>
> In 1979, AHA led a national boycott of the film *Heaven's Gate* to protest the film's cruelty to animals. The filmmakers had banned AHA from the set, where horses were tripped, one horse was blown up by dynamite, cattle and chickens were killed as props, and real cockfighting was performed. In 1980, as a result of the severe accusations regarding animal mistreatment and lack of safety for human actors while filming *Heaven's Gate*, AHA became part of the collective bargaining agreement with the Screen Actors Guild and the Alliance of Motion Picture and Television Producers. AHA's certified animal safety representatives would now be sent scripts in advance of filming and have access to productions where animals were used.

Viggo Mortensen, who starred in *Hidalgo*, claims he will not take a film that includes horses unless Rex is training them, because he knows Rex will ensure the horses' well-being and safety. Rex says about filming the movie, "I wanted to keep the horses safe, so I demanded that AHA [American Humane Association] safety representatives work on set with me in Morocco."

The horses Rex works with in films, television, and commercials live on his ranch. Between projects, they are ridden for roping cattle and do other types of ranch work as well as performing and competing in horse shows.

Hightower retired at Rex's farm and became a babysitter for the new colts. He always tried to jump in the trailer when Rex loaded up for a job, but later in his life, the work became too difficult for the horse's ailing body. When Rex pulled out with the trailer, Hightower would race around the field to show he was indignant at being left behind.

On October 30, 2008, at the age of twenty-six, Hightower died of natural causes and old age. He left Rex Peterson feeling heartbroken over the loss of such a great partner and friend.

Following in Rex's Footsteps

Rex inspired me by repeatedly demonstrating his ability to train horses to do what others would consider unachievable. People often ask of Rex's accomplishments, "How did you get the horse to do that?" Rex has taught me that, as in any good relationship, once you have trust, communication, respect, and knowledge, you can achieve almost anything. The best advice he ever gave me is that nothing is impossible when it comes to training horses. He opened my mind to believe that all horses improve with consistent and patient training. His knowledge, patience, and understanding give him access to the equine brain and how horses think.

Learning from and working with Rex helped me make training movie horses part of my career. I brought RJ to work on Ang Lee's *Taking Woodstock*, in which actor Jonathan Groff rode my horse. Ang Lee was so impressed with RJ's professionalism and skills that he asked, "Why can my horse hit his mark every time, and you actors cannot?" When the cameras roll, RJ lights up like every A-list Hollywood star.

Tips for Training Horses
from Rex Peterson

Teaching horses is like playing the piano. You have to learn every key. In the beginning, you must hunt for the keys. As time goes by, you know them individually. You play a chord and finally learn to play a song. Each note of the piano is equivalent to the individual movements of a horse, such as controlling the head or the hips or moving each foot independently. Put several of these movements together, and you have a chord. In the end, you are dancing with your horse and creating a song.

Each horse is an individual, and you must treat him as such. Be persistent in asking a horse to do something, but also patient enough to allow the horse to figure out the task you requested. Reward him so he knows he made the correct choice.

Tips for Training Horses
from Cari Swanson

There are many roads to Rome, so be open to trying different training techniques on each horse. Listen to your horse when you ask him to perform. If something is not working, try another avenue to unlock his mind.

Remember, horses' brains are in their feet. They are fight-or-flight animals, so always make sure you have a supple, obedient horse who will dance at any moment.

Let him know he did the right thing by praising with your calm voice and a reassuring hand on his neck.

Never, ever lose your temper.

Runaway Bride
An Unforgettable Experience with Hightower

Julia Roberts

It was a fabulous experience working with Hightower in *Runaway Bride*. But initially, it was very intimidating.

Rex Peterson, the horse's trainer, and Hightower had a very close bond. From the very beginning, I basically had to put my trust in both of them.

Julia Roberts trusting
Hightower and Rex

I was surprised and touched that it did not take long for Hightower to seem like a person to me.

Working with Rex and Hightower was an experience I will never forget. I fondly remember their professionalism and quiet command.

Chapter 3

RUSTY HENDRICKSON
(KALISPELL, MONTANA)
and HAILEE STEINFELD

Cimarron

Cimarron as Blackie, the Horse in *True Grit*
A Rugged Individual

Rusty Hendrickson

Charles Portis's novel *True Grit* was adapted into a film, released in 2010, that tells the story of a fourteen-year-old farmer's daughter, Mattie Ross (Hailee Steinfeld), and her quest to find Tom Chaney (Josh Brolin), her father's killer. She enlists the help of jaded alcoholic U.S. marshal Reuben J. "Rooster" Cogburn (Jeff Bridges) and Texas Ranger LaBoeuf (Matt Damon) to pursue Chaney on horseback through hostile Indian Nations territory.

Mattie's horse, Blackie, is played by Cimarron, my eight-year-old quarter horse. He's a tad standoffish and not like a responsive pet. If somebody wants to pet him, he'll have none of that. Cimarron has strong survival instincts and is a very rugged, tough individual. I own many other horses, including one from *Seabiscuit* and another from *Flicka*. They each have different personalities. Some horses are attention hogs. Not Cimarron. I understand that and like him the way he is. He's not high maintenance. Cimarron likes to please me and never wants to be scolded. After he gained trust in me as his trainer, he gave me anything I asked for, time after time.

While filming *3:10 to Yuma* in New Mexico, my team and I bought Cimarron from a local rancher. I had heard that the rancher raised horses who had the old, rare, and powerful Driftwood bloodline from both the sire and the dam. Cimarron's registered name is Driftswood. I'd wanted a Driftwood horse all my life. The original Driftwood was a bay stallion foaled in 1932 who gained fame because he was able to genetically pass on his outstanding qualities, such as stamina, toughness, and speed, to his progeny.

Second-Generation Horse Trainer

I trace my own lineage with horses to my father, Montana racehorse trainer Bud Hendrickson. When I was a teenager, I moved from Montana

36

to Kentucky to live with my mother and graduated with a degree in theology from Western Kentucky University. After college, I moved back to Montana, where I worked as a horseman in a trail-riding concession in Glacier National Park. After I'd worked a few years at the park, when a movie began filming there and the producers needed horses and wranglers, I got hired. I became convinced that working with horses in movies was what I wanted for a career. My wife, Debbie, and I, both in our twenties at the time, moved to Los Angeles so I could find horse work in the film industry.

I started working regularly in movies and television with jobs on *Little House on the Prairie* and the *Father Murphy* series. But I missed Montana. And I didn't want to raise our children in Hollywood. We took the chance that I could continue being hired for movies and television from our home in the Northwest. I bought the same trail-riding business where I'd gotten my first job. It kept us going until I was getting so much work casting and training horses for films that I could do the work full-time.

My big movie break was on *Dances with Wolves*, where I was head trainer and head wrangler. Before long, producers and directors were calling me regularly for help with their horse casting and action scenes.

"American Humane Association has fought hard to protect our four-legged performers through intensive on-set monitoring of films in production."

— **Clint Eastwood**, director and actor

I work with about seven or eight horses regularly. My crew, to whom I give equal credit for my success in over seventy movies, consists of Monty Stuart, Mark Warrack, my son Scout Hendrickson, and Lisa Brown. They have been the mainstay of my career for the past ten years.

One of the movies I am most satisfied with is *Seabiscuit*, where I was head wrangler. I'd worked a lot of Westerns, so this was my chance to do a racehorse film. I brought on horsemen I trusted to work the racetrack scenes. I hired Montana horsepeople as extras and for small roles. They also helped me find the right horses from around the country for playing fifteen-hand, 1,150-pound Seabiscuit and about fifty other horses in the movie.

The Right Horse for the Job

Any success I've had with horses I attribute not only to our team's good training techniques, but also to finding the right individual for the role. Cimarron is small and black, which is what the directors wanted. When I was hired to work on *True Grit*, I thought Cimarron would be a good fit because of his size and the fact that he could already do most of what was required in the script. Often, the scripts I receive for movies with horse action are the writers' imagined versions of what a horse can do. This script called for Blackie to swim across a river with a strong current in such a way that audiences will believe he'll get to the other side. We developed Cimarron's swimming skills for the role, and he did the scene successfully.

There was a lot of running and one scene when two people ride him through rough terrain. Had he not already been a ranch horse in rugged country, it wouldn't have worked. He had an upbringing that made him suited for the work. A horse without Cimarron's experience couldn't have accomplished the things Blackie needed to do for the story.

Cimarron doesn't have any nonsense about him. If I don't want him to go anywhere, he'll stand still. He's like riding a moped. He doesn't give more than I ask for, so he won't intimidate me or anyone else with too much horsepower. That's another quality that made him such a good choice as the horse for Hailee Steinfeld. She hadn't ridden before this movie and didn't need an overly energetic horse. Hailee developed affection for Cimarron while we gave her riding lessons. Although we had another horse as a double for Blackie, she was more comfortable with Cimarron.

Keeping Horses Safe

Everything Cimarron needed to do for the movie I thought out in advance. We prepped situations and made sure we weren't asking him to do anything that would hurt him. When hired for a movie, I work for the production company. I can't always dictate the relationship. That's when a good American Humane Association certified animal safety representative helps by insulating me from a boss who might unknowingly want me to do something that could be a safety issue for horse and rider. I appreciate that.

It took a long time getting Cimarron ready for *True Grit*. I broke each task into little steps, so he understood what I wanted him to do. He had a great deal of aptitude. In training sessions, I tried to push him to his limits and get as much endurance as I could. That way, I knew what point not to go past when we started filming.

We had done benchmark training with Cimarron by teaching him what I call a *laydown*. For a laydown, I work the ground to create a soft spot and lead the horse to lie down on that mark. The horse lets me crawl all over him even in this vulnerable situation. I walk between his legs and step over him. Laydown training had helped Cimarron learn to trust me. But for the role of Blackie, he had to do a horse fall that wasn't typical. The directors wanted Blackie to look as if he were being pulled by his bridle and his legs had given out under him.

To create the effect that Blackie was being pulled, the Rooster Cogburn stunt double, who worked with me, brought Cimarron to a mark, making it look as if Blackie had fallen forward. When Cimarron did a laydown and rolled on his back, it looked as if Blackie's legs had folded under him.

In a scene in which Blackie pulls Mattie out of the cavern where she's fallen, I was extremely proud of Cimarron. We prepped him, and he did it perfectly. We couldn't have asked for a better horse.

After *True Grit*

After *True Grit*, Cimarron worked with us on Quentin Tarantino's movie *Django Unchained*. He has an active life, although he's not always the featured or lead horse. Sometimes, he's in the background. In *Django Unchained*, he pulled a carriage. Cimarron is in the prime of his life now. He's part of our bag of tricks, a solid character. There's a place for him in most of the movies I do.

In between jobs, Cimarron works cattle at my ranch near Flathead Lake. I do recreational riding in the Swan Mountains with him. Cimarron also gets time off to just be a horse in the pasture, which he loves.

I feel affection for Cimarron and understand the horse's stoic nature. He's a gift from God.

Tips for Training Horses
from Rusty Hendrickson

It is not good to work or train horses with treats or cookies. When a horse is full, he will have no more motivation to perform the action. (My horses are very well fed, so they wouldn't work for food anyway.)

To gain a horse's trust, try using a pressure-and-release technique. Gently touch your finger to the horse's shoulder. The horse should have a mild reaction to being touched. The moment the horse reacts in any way, express kindness while calmly saying, "Good boy" or "Good girl." Continue giving the horse reassuring praise and approval. Because this is a positive technique, the horse will adjust to your touch.

A One-of-a-Kind Experience with Cimarron in *True Grit*

Hailee Steinfeld

My experience working with Cimarron on *True Grit* was truly one of a kind. Before we began principal shooting, I was given two weeks to get to know Cimarron and his personality.

Rusty Hendrickson and his team made me feel at ease and comfortable around Cimarron and really enhanced the experience. They taught me the tricks of bonding with a horse and guided me to becoming a great rider.

I gained an even greater respect for animals through this experience.

Hailee Steinfeld and Cimarron in *True Grit*

Part 2

BEARS, BIRDS, SNAKES, MONKEYS, AND OTHER ANIMAL STARS AND THEIR TRAINERS

Nicholas Toth and Casey the Bear

Some of the highlights while we were writing and doing research for *Animal Stars* involved spending time on film sets. We also visited places where animal actors live and are trained when they aren't working on projects. Each of us had memorable experiences that helped us better understand what is involved in keeping wild animals safe.

Robin Ganzert at *We Bought a Zoo*

When I visited film sets in Los Angeles shortly after becoming president and CEO of American Humane Association (AHA), I was amazed to see the number and quality of security measures taken. I was impressed with the top-notch, expensive, and permanent housing systems designed to provide shelter and protection for the animals in the movie.

I observed a scene on the set of *We Bought a Zoo* in which bears were brought to the set, housed in their own vehicle, and then sent home after they finished. A much smaller production crew worked when exotic animals entered. If you were not essential to that scene, you had to leave the set or even be removed. If you were essential crew, you were asked to step back and allow the animal trainer to do his work.

I noticed that security precautions heightened and focused when it came time for the bears to begin filming a scene. The AHA certified animal safety representatives constantly watched the bears for any stress signals or changes in breathing patterns. If the bears showed signs of anxiety, the AHA safety representatives

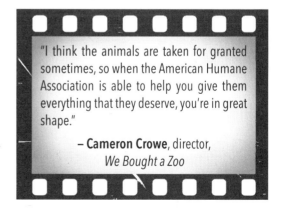

"I think the animals are taken for granted sometimes, so when the American Humane Association is able to help you give them everything that they deserve, you're in great shape."

– Cameron Crowe, director, *We Bought a Zoo*

stopped preparing for the scene. They tried to find out if there was any other information they needed or action that should be taken before moving forward.

The AHA safety representatives took note of environmental factors that could impact the well-being of bears, such as the set being too hot, cold, or cluttered with items that might injure animals. They interacted closely with the bears' trainer throughout the scene. The production crew deferred to the AHA safety representatives to make sure it was okay for them to continue.

Prior to the bears' arrival, meetings and discussions between the AHA safety representatives, trainers, and producers took place to ensure the animals' health and welfare. Everyone was intent on making sure everything would be safe. Even though the movie set was built on a temporary basis, the wild or exotic animals who stayed at the site had solid, safe housing that remained intact throughout filming.

When one of the bears performed, the set became utterly silent. I witnessed a beautiful respect for the bear and deep insight into the animal's intelligence. It was awe inspiring.

Allen and Linda at Working Wildlife

We have written a series of fifteen books celebrating human-animal companionship and connection. But when we drove north of Los Angeles to Working Wildlife's clean and well-tended facility, we weren't expecting to witness such endearing displays of affection between animal actors and their trainers. We had the pleasure of watching forty-year veteran trainer Steve Martin do his version of *Dances with Wolves*. Steve played with and was profusely licked on the face by wolves seen in *True Blood*, *The Vampire Diaries*, *Teen Wolf*, and *Game of Thrones*.

Awe inspiring and *beyond expectations* are good terms for describing what you are about to read in this section of *Animal Stars*. A capuchin monkey, a blue conure, a Burmese python, rare dog breeds, a northern black bear, a white-tailed deer, rex rabbits, gentoo penguins, and wolves will take you to places of movie magic. Join the crews on movie sets where

Steve Martin with a zebra
at Working Wildlife

these wild and exotic animals perform. In hushed silence, transport yourself in imagination to where animal descendants and inhabitants of jungles, forests, and ranches give all of us a glimpse into their magnificence.

Chapter 4

NICHOLAS TOTH

(PALMDALE, CALIFORNIA)

Casey the Bear

Casey as Baloo the Bear
in the *Jungle Book* Movies
Where's the Closest KFC?

Nicholas Toth

At the time I met the bear cub Casey, only two bears, whom we had taken in after they were abandoned, lived at my family's Cougar Hill Ranch, but they were too unpredictable to be good movie bears. My father, animal trainer George Toth, had helped Dennis "Doc" Casey find his first bears for Bear Country USA in South Dakota, so I called Dennis and told him we needed a new cub. After I flew to Bear Country USA, Dennis took me to see the park's thirty cubs.

Meeting Casey

I stood at the bear pen and watched the messy little baby bears squabble and tumble over each other. When I entered the pen, they all ran away. I planned to whittle down my choices to five cubs. Two of the babies started walking back in my direction. Casey was the first cub to make his way over to me. I had a handful of colored strings that I planned to use for identifying my choices. I wrapped a green string around Casey's neck. All the buildings at our ranch are painted green; maybe the green string was a sign of good things to come, but I did not pick the color with a special meaning in mind. Still, it was the one I grabbed for Casey from the choices in my hand.

Because Casey approached me so quickly, I thought, "You have some courage. You came up to me first." I sat in the pen for four hours and placed strings around the necks of four other bears. I planned to visit for five days while deciding which bear to take home.

While the other bears fought and played, I noticed that Casey often sat quietly in a corner. Three days into the visit, I decided to put leashes on the cubs and walk with them. Casey did not try to bite, but for about five minutes, he fought the idea of walking with me. Then he started getting into the rhythm of it. I admired his willingness to try a new experience.

The other bears snapped and bit at me all the time I stayed in their pen. Never Casey. By the third day, I had decided he would be our new bear. I returned on the fourth day of my visit and spent about fifteen minutes with the other bears. The rest of the visit, I focused on Casey. I called my aunt Helena and told her the good news that I had found the right bear. I named him Casey D. Bear. The initial *D* was for *Dennis*. When I brought the bear cub home from South Dakota, he was so tiny that he could have fit in a shoebox. We were all excited when Casey met everyone at Cougar Hill Ranch.

Before Casey

My ability to choose and train animals for films, television, and commercials came from having literally grown up with them. My father always wanted to be an animal trainer. He escaped from Hungary after the uprising against Russian rule in 1956. As a refugee, he immigrated to New York and soon made a name for himself training dogs. When I was only a baby, he moved to California and went to work for Disney Studios. In 1966, being an expert falconer, he was hired as an eagle trainer on the movie *Harpy*. He later worked on Ivan Tors's *Daktari*.

In October 1970, my father purchased Cougar Hill Ranch. Father had put me in movies working with animals starting when I was only four years old. But buying the ranch marked the formal beginning of my animal-training career. Our whole family was involved in the business. My mother, my sister Elizabeth Chamberlain, and my aunt Helena Walsh worked at the ranch. After Elizabeth and I came home from school each day, our chores included cleaning cages, feeding the animals, and taking out a couple of animals to work with.

When I was eight years old, Father gave Helena and me badgers to train for a movie. I spent time with them in a circus-type arena at the ranch. It was large enough for me to load the badgers into a crate and release them so that they could move around, yet small enough for me to tame them. While Elizabeth worked with otters, I trained the badgers, trying not to get bitten. Even though Helena and I worked with the badgers for a couple of years, I thought it was remarkable that we were each only bitten once. The badgers were very smart, and I learned a lot about them. To this day, as far as I know, nobody has investigated badgers as thoroughly as Helena and I did back then.

From Badgers to Bears

In 1997, Elizabeth, Helena, and I inherited Cougar Hill Ranch. Our first bear, the incredible Moscow, starred in a Disney movie released in 1979, titled *The North Avenue Irregulars*. In one scene, all of us — Moscow, snakes, geese, and swans — were in the backseat of a car that appeared to crash. All the animals bolted from the car, but Moscow stayed. While I was in college, the talented and fearless Moscow died of natural causes.

My childhood and young adult time with animals had given me the foundation I needed to bond with Casey, the bear who would change my life. As Casey grew from cub to adolescence, he impressed me by being a fast learner who loved to work. He had an ego and could be quite a show-off. If he missed his mark on set, it was never necessary to correct him. He knew it, and the mistake embarrassed him.

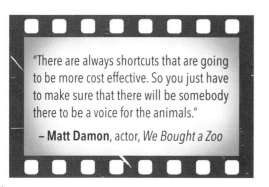

"There are always shortcuts that are going to be more cost effective. So you just have to make sure that there will be somebody there to be a voice for the animals."

– Matt Damon, actor, *We Bought a Zoo*

The younger Casey was social with people. As he aged, he became less friendly. Later in life, the only two people he really loved were Elizabeth and me. But after my sister got pregnant and took a leave of absence for a few weeks, Casey would have nothing to do with her. He did the same with my wife, Kari, ignoring her after she had our son and came back to work.

Most black bears have tiny ears and dark muzzles. Casey had big ears and a golden muzzle. He also had a lot of character. Showing a good sense of humor, he allowed us to do silly things, such as dressing him up in clothes and wrapping wristwatches around his arms. The wristwatches became one of his trademark images when he did a Seiko watch ad.

Casey's Career and KFC

When Casey was only five months old, he got his first job on a television series in Canada. We flew there together. I had to go to the cargo hold to pick up my baby bear. The attendant in charge seemed to only speak French, but when he saw Casey, he asked, "You have a baby bear?" I commented about his sudden ability to speak English. He said, "In Quebec, we only speak French." Casey had surprised him so much that he blurted out his question in English.

Casey started getting bigger parts in movies and television. After filming *Back to the Future*, we had a barbecue at the ranch. At this time, Casey was younger and still social enough to allow people to take pictures with him. Somebody brought a bucket of Kentucky Fried Chicken (KFC) and gave him a piece. He lit up as if saying, "This is the best thing on earth!" Casey's daily intake of food was two five-gallon buckets of a mixture of lettuce, apples, peaches, oranges, berries, melons, breads, carrots, and our homemade dog food composed of chicken soup mixed with kibble. In the winter, he ate only one bucket.

He enjoyed and thrived on his regular food, but while some bears like sweets as treats, Casey didn't care much for them. Instead, his true love turned out to be KFC. We always had to look for the location of the KFC closest to whatever site we were working on. It could *only* be chicken from KFC. No other fried chicken satisfied him. When working on location, we drove as much as an hour and a half to a KFC, even if there was another restaurant that sold chicken just down the street from the set. If the chicken was a day old, Casey knew. The fresher the better. And we had to bring him Colonel Sanders's Original Recipe. He could tell the difference and refused any substitute. We deboned the chicken and gave it to him. Then he would reach his big paw into the bucket. The KFC chicken smelled so good that we had to make sure that a hungry film crew didn't steal Casey's stash.

Another of Casey's preferences was to drink only spring water, so we brought thirty gallons of spring water to the set. If we had to stay longer and our supply ran out, the producers would purchase more. "This is for a bear?" people would ask.

Helena Walsh and Casey

When we were doing the movie version of the *Beverly Hillbillies* television series, we were in the town of Fort Ross, California. The crew had constructed a set for Casey to do a wrestling scene with my wife, Kari. I tried to explain Casey's demands to the production company as similar to the dictates of a diva. The nearest KFC was eighty miles from the movie set. Every morning, the producers had to send a driver to KFC to bring back a bucket for Casey. The store didn't open until ten o'clock in the morning, so it was about 11:30 AM when the crew member arrived back on set with Casey's chicken. We always saved a little stash from the previous day, in case we had to start filming early, so we could attempt to stave off Casey's hunger with day-old chicken.

People never complained about Casey's unusual requirements after they saw him work. They realized that meeting his demands was well worth it. He never failed on a job. On one site, five setups were completely changed for what was supposed to be one day of shooting. For each take, everything on the set would be different from how it was the last time Casey saw it. Someone asked, "So, do you think Casey can do this today?" Casey amazed everyone by working all five setups in one day.

We built a pen for Casey at the ranch so he could roam around in a larger space. He learned many tricks there that later looked great on film. He learned to roll a large log. We trained him to knock down a beehive for one of the *Jungle Book* movies. While we trained and played with him in the yard, he exercised his talent for being a major deal maker. During our training sessions, watermelon or a cookie would work as a cold date, but KFC was our version of a hot date.

Casey and *Rudyard Kipling's The Jungle Book*

On *Rudyard Kipling's The Jungle Book*, the director, Stephen Sommers, was having problems with the bears originally cast for the part of Baloo the Bear. Stephen asked if Casey could try out for the role in one of the night shots. Since Casey was a North American black bear, and Baloo the Bear was supposed to be a brown bear, the producers were using brown bears. We experimented with spray makeup to turn Casey into a brown bear. We diluted nontoxic paint that young children use in school art classes for finger painting. It sticks to hair and can be washed off with water. For a week, we tried using different levels of dilutions to find the right mixture of water and finger paint that would transform a black bear into a brown bear.

On each day of the shoot, we brought Casey to the set two hours early. We poured our premixed paint into a portable sprayer. We paid (rewarded) him for letting us apply his makeup by Helena feeding him constantly, while I got to be the artist. Each day, it took at least two hours to transform him into a brown bear. He loved it and had fun with all the attention. Big fans were set up in his trailer to keep him cool. He came to understand exactly what we were doing. He would lie back and lift up one arm, then the other arm, as we sprayed brown makeup all over his body. Then we had to wait for the paint to dry.

Bridgestone/Firestone Centennial Wilderness owned a ranch in Tennessee near Sparta. While we filmed the movie in Sparta, all the animals in the film stayed at the ranch. After every day's shoot, we took Casey for a swim in the ranch's pool to wash off the paint until it completely dissolved.

Casey's Star Accommodations

Although other animals might stay at the ranch, while we filmed on location, we never left Casey at a movie site. Each night, he went back with us to the lodge where we were staying. He slept in a trailer we parked at a specially assigned space outside our room, not twenty feet from the front door. We would peek in and check on him, to make sure he was comfortable. The trailer was like his den — his home away from home. We built a special large case, like a box, inside Casey's trailer with plenty of bedding, and he loved sleeping in it. We often found him in the morning, buried under the straw bedding with his nose poking out. One of the veterinarians at the *Jungle Book* site commented on our high level of dedication and devotion to Casey.

In Tennessee, there were massive, crazy storms that rampaged through Sparta. One night, a mind-blowing storm whipped through with well over a hundred lightning strikes in a short period of time. Our wolf, Shannon, and Casey were okay, since we had them with us at the lodge and housed in nice places. We had brought a camper shell and installed it in the truck to create a safe and perfect wolf's den. On stormy nights, we parked the trailer lengthwise next to our room, only twenty steps away, so we could repeatedly check on Casey and Shannon.

Casey wound up doing 80 percent of the bear work on *The Jungle Book*. He pulled off the part of Baloo the Bear so well that he even got cast credit. Shannon the wolf got cast credit, too. This movie experience was especially meaningful to me because it happened a few years after my father died. If anyone had been wondering whether Cougar Hill

Ranch could continue without George Toth at the helm, on that film, Casey made a believer out of a lot of people. His success as Baloo the Bear demonstrated that we were here to stay.

One other detail about Casey in *The Jungle Book* is especially important to my family and me. Three days into the movie's filming, Casey, in full brown-bear makeup, did a major scene for director Stephen Sommers, who declared, "Casey *is* Baloo." When the animal coordinator for the movie cast Casey for *The Jungle Book*, I requested benefits. My wife and I were thinking about starting a family, and I wanted health and hospital insurance. Kari and I put the insurance to good use when my wife became pregnant. I always say that I wouldn't have my son today if not for Casey. That is how much this bear changed my life.

Casey's Star Personality

Casey loved to stretch his feet up and have us scratch them. He would let us know when he'd had enough pampering by playfully knocking me down only one minute after a nice feet-scratching session. His other game was to play catch. He had several balls that were his favorites for tossing.

Casey did not like other bears, especially babies. If he sniffed a cub, he looked disgusted at the odor and did not want to go near where the baby bear had been. We had to spray the area with Febreze in an attempt to get rid of baby-bear odor.

With all his endearing qualities, Casey was, like other bears, fast and smart, and he could be extremely aggressive. We knew that. Occasionally, we would look at him and say, "He is thinking evil." Sometimes, he was simply frustrated. He rarely made a noise, but if he did, we knew it was time for him to take a break.

Because of Winn-Dixie was a fun project to do with Casey. In one scene, he was supposed steal Leo Tolstoy's classic novel *War and Peace* from the town's library. Then he had to carry the book to a tree and read it. Weighing in at over a thousand pages, the book was heavy. Casey didn't like having to pull it off a library shelf with his mouth and bring it to the tree, so we hollowed out a chunk to make it lighter. He clutched the full book in his paw during the scene while he sat under the tree and read it.

It was ninety-three degrees on the Monday when the scene was scheduled to film. The library scene required Casey to maneuver in a very tight space, and I knew that hot weather would affect his performance. So I asked the director if we could push the shoot to Tuesday. Everyone was astounded by how well Casey performed during the cooler weather on Tuesday.

Casey loved his mark. Sometimes, we would have to do work-aways in which I gave him direction and then had to move from camera range or out of his sight. In a work-away, the animal is not facing the trainer and is sent to a spot, or mark, with the trainer behind instead of in front of him. Animals must be intelligent to do work-aways. Casey was so smart that he could hit his mark without any of us being on set.

During one movie shoot that took place in the middle of winter, it started raining. I said, "Casey does not work in the rain, especially in the winter."

Everyone said, "Do you mean we have to work around the bear's schedule?"

I replied, "He will not come outside if it is raining. He will stay in his trailer."

And that's exactly what he did.

Good-Bye, Casey

As Casey got older, movie work became less enjoyable for him. At the age of twenty-three, after his last film, *Evan Almighty*, he retired and didn't work for two years. He would hibernate during colder weather, come out to eat, and go back into his box to hibernate some more.

When Casey died, all of us were upset. I had known there was something special about him from the first day, when he was one of only two cubs who came back to me after initially running away. He always nudged me in the right direction. We had an understanding between us that transcended anything else I've ever experienced. He knew how to play me, and he let me play him. Always a professional, he inherently knew exactly what to do and not do on sets and loved the work. I miss Casey every day.

The day Casey passed, my son was with me. For the first time, I told him that Casey was the reason we had been able to afford to have him come into this world. Casey had made a fundamental and important change in my life that is hard for me to put into words. We had a brotherhood and sense of sharing our world together in such a profound way. I will never have that kind of relationship with another bear.

Tips for Comfortably and Safely Transporting Large Animals from Nicholas Toth

There were several things I always did with Casey that I think are especially important for transporting large animals. If we had a long travel day ahead, we put extra bedding, support, and padding in the trailer for him.

Every time we travel with animals or insects, I check the weather for driving conditions ahead of us, and what might affect the shoot, such as heavy winds for a commercial that involves using butterflies.

We always have our vehicles inspected before each trip. The mechanic checks everything, including the tires. The last thing anyone wants to have happen is to break down in the middle of a long trip with animals.

We bring plenty of food for the animals, and their medications, since a veterinarian might not be nearby. We include flea and bug spray. I pack at least three toolboxes and a change of clothes that is not in the suitcase.

My mom had a habit of blessing our truck with holy water and saying a prayer with us before we left the ranch for our trips to work locations. My mom and Helena always said very long blessings. When I do them now, they are much shorter: "Take us there. Bring us back. Amen."

Hollyberry as a Deer on *NCIS* and *The Mentalist*
The Indestructible Deer

Nicholas Toth

We've all seen the image of a deer's frozen stare as a car hurtles toward the animal on a dark and stormy night. None of us would ever want to witness the deer (or driver) being hurt or killed. While making movies, television shows, and commercials, my deer walk away from these kinds of "accidents" all the time. And the deer who I like to say "has been 'hit by a car' and lived to tell about it so many times" is one who actually wouldn't have survived without love and care from my family and me.

At Cougar Hill Ranch, we provide and train animals for film, television, and educational purposes. The California Department of Fish and Wildlife often brings us wild or exotic animals who need to be rehabilitated. Most of the animals we take in and keep will never be able to survive in nature again due to poor health, injury, or disability.

One day, a warden brought a day-old baby doe to our facility. An officer had found her near the highway. She was so extremely tiny that she fit into the palm of my hand. We theorized that her small size might have been due to having been born prematurely. Dehydrated and malnourished, the baby was not doing well. We worked to save her life, feeding her every two hours. In about a week, her health stabilized, and she started walking. In a month, she was relatively healthy, although still small.

Anytime we keep a baby deer, we give him or her a forest name, such as Forest or Aspen. We gave this small deer the name Hollyberry after the bush, with its slick green leaves and crimson berries, that is so popular during the holiday season. We just call her Holly.

In all the time we have raised and trained rescued animals to work in film, we have never kept one in our house any longer than necessary. That way, if the animal can survive injuries, he or she might not be too

Hollyberry

domesticated to return to the wild. Because Holly was so tiny and frail, she lived in our home longer than most. Consequently, she bonded with us, as we did with her. Holly became part of our family. Everybody loved this gentle creature with beautiful blue eyes.

Touching Holly

We taught Holly how to lie down on our couch. If she became too active, we let her have a time-out there. Deer paw the ground before lying down, so with hand scratches, we imitated pawing like a deer on the couch. Following our lead, she too pawed the sofa and started viewing it as a place where she could sprawl out and rest. When we scratched the couch, she lay down on it, and we gave her a bottle of goat's milk.

Because of how we raised her, Holly has no fear of human touch. She lets everybody pet her. As a key member of an educational program we provide, Holly used to travel to classrooms. Not the type of deer who runs away, she stayed calm and showed everyone her laid-back nature. Before she came into a classroom, we carefully placed mats on the floor so Holly would not slip. She stood, as we talked with the kids and told them about her life and habits. Many of the children had seen the same type of deer from a distance, so they were curious about her.

Each year in our community, Holly is invited to Christmas pageants to help with fund-raising activities. People take pictures with children sitting by her. We are careful to keep kids who are too excited or active from hurting her.

Training Holly

Since Holly stayed with us while her health improved, we trained her to work on projects that called for deer animal actors. We used a bottle to train her. When she saw her bottle, she got excited. At first, she drank goat's milk from the bottle. Then we started diluting the milk. By the time we reached a ten-to-one ratio, there was a mild taste of the goat's milk, but it was almost all water. We no longer feed her with a bottle.

A bell ringing and a buzzer clicking cued Holly to come to her mark for a treat. She loves finding and staying on her mark without walking around. One time, she had to stand on her mark for three hours next to a man near a tree. She didn't seem to mind it at all.

Not only do animals have to be comfortable on set, but they also must be able to travel to and from locations. Holly likes riding in our trailer or van, and she jumps into it right away, ready and eager to go to work. For local trips, we take her in our van. If we are going a long distance or staying for a period of time at a production site, we bring her in a trailer so she can have more room. We take her out on walks several times a day.

When she was a baby, Holly traveled a lot. We made sure that she and our other animals had fun meeting children at schools as well as the people on sets. If it isn't fun for the animals, they forget that working is something they want to do.

My concept of fun is to only give encouragement — to my animals and also to our son. I go to my son's events and support him. I do not criticize or say, "Why did you not do better?" I am the same with my animals. I never make them feel bad if they did something wrong or their performance wasn't perfect.

Deer in Danger

The combination of Holly's place in our family, the positive nature of my training methods, and her calm nature has made her excel at depicting the iconic scenes of a deer in danger. When we take her to a film shoot, she watches a car coming toward her at fifty miles per hour. She stands still while the car approaches, with absolute certainty and trust that we will make sure she does not get hit.

In *Terminator 3: Rise of the Machines*, a motorcycle crash in the movie involved two deer. Holly played one of them. The other was a running deer, so naturally, she ran away from the vehicle. Holly stood during the fake accident as if she were saying, "Okay, I don't care." She remained relaxed about all the action that took place while filming. And there was a lot of action in that movie!

When Holly works on a show, commercial, or movie, people tend to remember and ask for her by name. They want her to come back, and she is cast often.

Keeping Holly Safe

With all the different ideas that come to us for animal work, we discuss what is and is not possible. Holly is the only deer in the industry who has her own animatronic double. Animatronics is like a fancy puppet replica of an animal, plant, or creature that moves and appears to be physically realistic. We built animatronic Holly for a commercial in which a deer looks lifeless after a car crash. Animatronic Holly prevents real Holly from doing anything that might be dangerous.

Before we do any action involving Holly and a car, American Humane Association (AHA) safety representatives and I always speak with the stunt driver and director. We lay down the guidelines: "If you want the car to stop within ten feet of the deer, the car can drive twenty miles per hour. If you want the car to stop twenty feet from the deer, you can drive up to thirty miles per hour. If you drive forty miles per hour, the car must stop thirty feet from where the deer is standing. The faster you come at the deer, the sooner you have to stop." By taking all these precautions, we have conditioned Holly to know that she will be safe. Every shoot has to be done in a way that does not threaten the animal. I have never put her or any other deer in danger.

One night, we were doing a tire commercial on a rainy road. The AHA representatives were very concerned about the wet conditions. We managed to work out an agreement with the production people that made everybody happy. Instead of placing Holly and the other deer in the middle of the road, we stood them on the side closest to the trainers. This made it only look as if Holly was in front of the oncoming car.

Holly's Television Triumphs

I am especially proud of the work Holly did on the television series *NCIS* in 2011 for a segment called "Tell-All." In it, a couple drives down a country road and sees a deer. They get out their camera to take a picture, and the deer walks down a trail away from them. The couple follows the deer, and Holly leads them to a body in the grass. The victim is a commander with the Defense Intelligence Agency, so the Naval Criminal Investigative Service (NCIS) gets involved in solving the crime.

> **DID YOU KNOW...?**
>
> In 1976, a bigger, and definitely badder, King Kong arrived back in New York in the form of a forty-foot-tall animatronic ape.

The scene with Holly was in the introduction to the show and a major plot point. All the grips, directors, camera people, and film crew were trying to figure out how they were going to shoot it. It turned out to be an all-day event.

The producer asked me about Holly, "Can she do this today? In one day? I only have a day."

I answered, "Yes, Holly can do this scene in one day. She will walk down the trail to the body."

Holly did everything the producer wanted. I only needed to show her where she should walk and give her encouragement. We coordinated the crew's timing and ours. We shot the scene in one day with no rehearsals.

In the third season of *The Mentalist*, in 2010, in the episode "Red Moon," Holly charmed Simon Baker, the star and director of that episode.

Simon's character, Patrick Jane, meets a deer (Holly) as he walks through an orchard. He and the deer have a moment of connection before the deer walks away. It wasn't originally written that way, though. Simon was only supposed to spot a wild deer running past him. But Holly liked Simon and kept trying to go over to him. So they rewrote the script. Instead of Holly running, as if from a hunter, they had Holly and Patrick stop to exchange meaningful glances, which added a note of mystery to the plot.

It's usually easy to have Holly work *with* her friendly nature instead of *against* it, as she did with her new friend Simon Baker. But for one project, it was funny trying to keep her from doing what comes naturally. In the scene, she was supposed to stand in a garden full of fresh vegetation. The director did not want her to eat, and we tried to stop her. But Holly yearned to chew the scenery. She was really acting by not eating the entire contents of that garden.

Aging Holly

Holly is currently fourteen years old and continues to live a comfortable life. As she ages, she can no longer handle the cold winter months, and she gets chilled. At night, she likes going into her own little trailer to sleep. At dusk each evening, we make sure Holly is comfortable inside it.

Nicholas Toth with Hollyberry, waiting for Helena Walsh to give her an apple

We buy and cut Holly's food especially for her. She is a picky eater. Normally, we feed her a mix of apples, chopped carrots, and bananas. We add strawberries and peaches, but not too many. She also eats veggies, a special deer grain, and a mix of different kinds of hay. She loves to eat and nibble on green grass and natural vegetation, but this type of food is not good for her. So we sometimes use a safe product named Deer Off that protects gardens from deer foraging. On a production, using Deer Off makes Holly eat her food and not the local vegetation.

I cannot begin to express how different Holly is compared to most deer. She is a good thinker and has the brainpower to perform. Plus, she is sweet. Most deer don't have both sweetness and intelligence. She always hits her mark. People are surprised at how well she works. She consistently comes through for us. We have other deer who will be with us for the rest of their lives, since they cannot be released into the wild, even if they are not suited for work as animal actors. Holly pays for their keep with the work she does so skillfully.

Every once in a while, Holly has a couple of bad days. But mostly, she is doing well as a healthy senior citizen. Holly will retire and live with our family until she leaves us to go to a heavenly garden where she can munch on fresh greens to her heart's content. She is a deer/dear in every sense of the word. The fact that she would stand on a spot in the road, look at a car speeding toward her, and trust me to never let her get hurt is one of the most satisfying and humbling aspects of my many years of training animal actors.

Tips for Rescuing a Distressed Animal in Nature from Nicholas Toth

If you find injured wildlife, call a state or county agency first and find out if there are people who are licensed to care for injured wildlife. Do not try to feed the animal anything. Put the animal in a box and drape a towel over it to keep the box dark. Then take the animal to a licensed wildlife rehabilitation facility.

Chapter 5

THOMAS GUNDERSON
(LOS ANGELES, CALIFORNIA)

Crystal Picasso, painting

Crystal as the Capuchin
in *Night at the Museum* and *We Bought a Zoo*
I *Am* a Monkey's Uncle

Thomas Gunderson

Crystal the Monkey, as she is known by her fans, is no ordinary primate; she's an animal actor. Although the term *animal actor* tends to gain more respect, to put it more accurately, she's more of an animal "reactor," responding to verbal cues and hand signals. Animals like Crystal are dynamic, interactive, and essential components in the film and television industry. Unlike human actors, Crystal is a monkey and doesn't pretend to be anything else. She doesn't immerse herself in a role or have to memorize any lines. What you see on the screen is very organic.

I am Crystal's trainer, caretaker, coworker, and adoptive uncle. She was two and a half years old when we met, and we've been together for a little over seventeen years. I needed to come up with a name for Crystal that was unique within the company where I work. At the time, I was into country music, and on one occasion, when I was thinking about what I wanted to name her, a Crystal Gayle song played on my truck radio. Soon after, I worked at an American Veterinary Medical Association conference and was invited to attend their big dinner. The evening's entertainer was Crystal Gayle. I liked the name, and the coincidence cemented my decision.

The journey to training Crystal and other animal actors began with my strong, lifelong attraction to all animals and a particular interest in primates. I was born in Albert Lea, Minnesota, and lived my early years in the city of Twin Lakes and on a working farm outside Austin, Minnesota. My family moved to a rural home near Arlington, Nebraska, where I stayed until graduating from high school. As far back as I can remember, I wanted to work with animals and have them live in my house. Watching the original *Doctor Dolittle* with Rex Harrison inspired me to become a veterinarian. After working with a vet for a few years in high school, I noticed that most of his patients didn't necessarily want to be around him, due to certain examination procedures, treatments, and vaccinations. I decided to switch professions and go into zoo keeping.

My aunt, who lived in the Los Angeles area, found out about the Exotic Animal Training and Management (EATM) Program at Moorpark College in Moorpark, California, where students learn about animals and prepare for jobs involving them. At the EATM program, I discovered I was on the right path to a fulfilling career. It's also where I met my beautiful wife, Stacy.

Upon graduation, Stacy got a job with Birds and Animals Unlimited, a prominent and successful movie animal–training company based in Los Angeles with resources worldwide. I took a position as an elephant keeper/trainer at the San Diego Wild Animal Park near Escondido. Stacy and I maintained our long-distance relationship for three years until it was time to find work closer to each other. I joined Birds and Animals Unlimited, and both of us started working at the Animal Actors Stage Show, Universal Studios Hollywood. I worked there for twelve and a half years until we decided to get married and start a family. I left the show but continued to do movie-studio work. Stacy quit her job to stay home with the children.

Crystal at Home

Life with our growing children and Crystal the Monkey is an adventure. At just under two feet tall and a little over six pounds, this pint-size primate is an audience gatherer and crowd-pleaser. People of all ages light up when they meet her. Whenever we go out in public, I have to allow extra time to answer questions, pose for photos, and maybe even let Crystal sign an autograph or two. Although she loves to draw, her penmanship leaves a lot to be desired.

I take advantage of such encounters to teach a little about wildlife conservation and why monkeys don't make good pets. I mention that Crystal's predominantly mellow personality is atypical. Monkeys are messy eaters, go to the bathroom whenever and wherever they please, and are more into *de*struction than *con*struction. They tend to bite when frustrated, frightened, or trying to exert their dominance. I also tell people who gather to meet Crystal that her needs will be met for the rest of her life, but I ask them to think about monkeys in the wild. Humans are threatening their existence through hunting, encroaching on their habitats, and introducing diseases for which they have no immunity.

Stacy and I have two children, Jaden and Logan, ages eight and ten, respectively. Crystal shares our home with another capuchin, also a female, named Squirt. Although the monkeys are free to roam about, they do have to follow a few simple rules: don't destroy, don't steal, and don't get on the tables or kitchen counters unless invited. The monkeys get frequent baths and wear diapers when inside. Capuchins have a nasty habit of urinating on their hands and feet and then wiping the pungent fluid all over their fur. There are a few theories as to why they do this; I believe that the behavior helps repel insects and some external parasites.

Crystal and Squirt are closely bonded to each other, as well as to my family. One way they demonstrate affection is through grooming — a social behavior with the primary purpose of removing external parasites

From left to right: Stacy, Jaden, Thomas, Crystal, and Logan Gunderson at home

and debris from the fur and cleaning wounds on the skin. They frequently groom us, even though we shower daily and don't have fleas or ticks. They even take care of the dogs, primarily when they're napping. It used to startle the dogs to wake up to the monkeys grooming them, but now they're accustomed to it.

By California law, monkeys have to be provided with outdoor enclosures. Spending time together outdoors also gives Crystal and Squirt a break from humans. They share a roomy estate completely furnished with large tree branches, vines, swings, tube tunnels, and toys. Their house is equipped with insulated walls and double-paned, acrylic windows. This is where they retire to have a little monkey-mischief time without any rules.

At night, the two monkeys have a few options for where they can sleep. Their preferred choice is to share our bed. They love to cuddle, almost to the point of suffocating Stacy and me. Their second choice is a hammock suspended from one of the wooden rails at the top of our lodgepole bed. Last is a very comfortable dog bed on the floor. Since monkeys instinctively prefer to sleep in trees for safety, the floor probably makes them feel vulnerable.

Crystal definitely relishes her sleep, so I make sure she gets to bed early the night before we are going on a job. After I'm done packing the truck and getting myself ready the next morning, I rouse her out of bed. It only takes about five minutes before we can leave for work.

Monkeys are very high maintenance, and their curious nature can get them into a lot of trouble. We like to stimulate Crystal by providing puzzle containers filled with healthy snacks, like nuts and sunflower seeds. She gets especially excited about toddler activity centers with all sorts of buttons, levers, and switches that activate various lights and sounds. If she's sitting in someone's lap, she'll often play with the zipper on the person's jacket or sweatshirt.

Crystal at Work

Crystal really seems to enjoy working. I think that's because she gets to exercise her body and mind. In addition to performing in front of large audiences at Universal Studios for nearly seven years, Crystal has appeared in over twenty feature films, four independent films, three television movies, more than thirty domestic television shows, four foreign television shows, six commercials, three music videos, dozens of photo shoots, six promotional events, three award shows, two fund-raisers for charity, and one public service announcement. She is registered with the Internet Movie Database (IMDb.com), is documented on *Wikipedia* and YouTube, and has her own fan club and Facebook page established by some of her admirers. To my knowledge, she's the first animal to ever have a manager. Is her star on the Hollywood Walk of Fame or her footprints in front of Grauman's Chinese Theatre? Not yet.

When we're on set, Crystal stays with me and never in a crate or cage. I make sure she always has a fresh diaper. I've probably changed more diapers than any parent in history, and the number is still climbing. She's used to wardrobe fittings but has only worn makeup once — for *Night at the Museum: Battle of the Smithsonian.* We applied a nontoxic yellow grease paint to the top of her head, giving her a "skunk stripe"

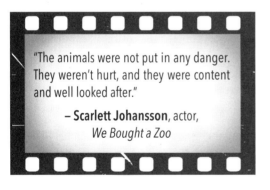

"The animals were not put in any danger. They weren't hurt, and they were content and well looked after."

– **Scarlett Johansson**, actor,
We Bought a Zoo

to change her appearance as the character Able the astronaut monkey. Usually, she's cast as a male character, so she rarely gets to show off her feminine side.

Her favorite treats are yogurt, berry-flavored applesauce, grapes, nuts, sunflower seeds, and Nutella. Her favorite nuts are pistachios. Crystal genuinely endorsed the product in a "Get Crackin'" commercial for Wonderful Pistachios. In the piece, she appears to be attending a movie premiere and is revealed walking down a green carpet, wearing a lime-green dress and sporting a jeweled purse filled with pistachio nuts.

Preparing Crystal for work on a set involves two types of training. First, I teach her specific behaviors she has to learn for the project. Second, I habituate her to the environment. With both tasks, I start out slowly. As she shows progress, I build a little bit more into the behavior. In trainer lingo, this is called successive approximation.

For example, if I'm going to teach Crystal to climb a ladder, I start by setting her at the top and paying her with one of her favorite treats. Then I place her on the second step from the top and ask her to climb up to the top step with some guidance. As soon as she makes it to the top step, I pay her again. I repeat this process until she no longer needs my help to climb to the top of the ladder. Once she is confident in moving up from the second step to the top, I do the same process with the third step down from the top and so on. I also use successive approximation to desensitize Crystal to all the people and equipment on set, so nothing is unfamiliar to her. If there is an element that might scare her, I take more time getting her used to it so she doesn't get stressed.

There is a scene in *The Hangover Part II* in which Crystal's character rides on a motorcycle with two stuntmen. One of them fires a gun as they speed down an alley. I've had Crystal riding on my ATV for years, so I knew that wouldn't be a problem. For the gunfire, I started out by clapping two boards together; then I fired a cap gun; and finally, I used the sound of a starter pistol. She was fully prepared for the scene by the time we got to filming.

Crystal's Safety

Safety for the animals, cast, and crew is paramount. If something is too risky, we always find a way to get the shot without putting Crystal, or any other animal, in harm's way. For example, there is a scene in Disney's *Treasure Buddies* in which Crystal strikes a wooden match and lights a hurricane lantern. My cotrainer, Tony Suffredini, and I prepped those two behaviors for over a month. We wanted to make sure Crystal was proficient before we added the element of fire. After she was ready to do the scene safely, we coated her arm in fire retardant and stayed no more than two feet away in case we had to extinguish the match. She pretended to light the lantern; we handed her the match and lit it for her (she never lit it on her own). She touched the lit match to the wick successfully every time. The film used visual effects, or computer-generated imagery (CGI), to create the lantern's flame. Sometimes, we have to rely on animatronics and CGI technologies, which have really advanced, to give the audience a sense of reality on film while keeping the animals safe on set.

In the movie *The Hangover Part II* Crystal had to appear to be smoking. The visual effects department did a fantastic job of providing the flame for the lighter, the lit end of a fake cigarette, and the smoke. My job was to teach her how to manipulate the props and make the appropriate facial expressions. When we put it all together, it looked very real. The scene caused quite an uproar when the director, Todd Phillips, joked about Crystal becoming addicted to cigarettes. He loved Crystal and never asked her to actually smoke. Besides, based on my ethical principles, I would never train or even allow any animal to smoke.

Animal safety is always essential to me. In numerous media interviews, I have been asked about my perspective on having American Humane Association (AHA) safety representatives on set. I believe that only unscrupulous trainers would have a problem with the representatives. They are obviously there to protect the animals. I take advantage of their presence by asking them to assist me in watching out for potential hazards that I might miss. For example, we might not see a loose dog who could try to interfere or a cat who could be a distraction when we're on location. AHA safety reps also help protect our reputations, as well as those of the production companies, by documenting how we were able to achieve certain shots when it appeared that the animal was injured or stressed.

Crystal's Unique Talents and Experiences

After all our years together, I am still amazed by Crystal. There have been numerous times during training or in the middle of a scene when she has made her own decision about what to do, and her choice was even better than I could have expected. It's all her; I can't take credit for it. The set of *Superhero Movie* provides an excellent example of her improvisational skills. One scene revealed a small crowd gathered around a monkey who was dancing for tips. People were to take turns dropping money into a hat that was placed just a foot away from Crystal. During one take, someone threw a dollar bill that missed the target and landed in front of Crystal. Without skipping a beat, she picked up the dollar with her foot, passed it to her hand, set it in the hat, and continued to dance. Everyone was totally impressed, including me.

Crystal has traveled throughout the United States (including Hawaii) and Canada. She's even been to Thailand. She continues to have unique experiences, like flying in business class on an airplane. Her résumé proves she's worked alongside talented and famous actors. In fact, her costars have often doted on her. While waiting for an appearance on the show *Home and Family*, Betty White offered Crystal the comfort of her air-conditioned trailer. Jason Patric did the same when Crystal visited the set of *My Sister's Keeper*. Actress JoAnna Garcia Swisher brought Crystal toys to play with during downtime while we were making NBC's *Animal Practice*.

During the filming of *Night at the Museum*, Robin Williams preferred to visit with Crystal between takes rather than watch his own performance on the monitor. He even signed a poster-sized "Thank you and farewell" card created by the entire cast and crew. Upon completion of her last scene in the movie, everyone cheered and presented Crystal with the card and a fancy cake. Laughter filled the soundstage when I let her dive headfirst into her dessert.

Tips for Training Animals from Thomas Gunderson

No matter what kind of animal you're going to train, I recommend following five important pieces of advice. First, try to work with your animal when you're in a good mood. Animals can usually sense your emotional state, so you want to be very positive.

Second, set aside plenty of time so you don't have to rush the session. You may have to spend a bit more time than you expected, trying to fix something the animal doesn't understand.

Third, keep your sessions short, at least in the beginning. Animals typically can't focus their attention for very long, so only train for about five to ten minutes. Try to end on a positive note. Everyone, even an animal, likes to walk away a winner.

Fourth, be consistent. Consistency is probably the most important tip I can give. Make sure your verbal and hand cues are the same from session to session. The criteria you set for each behavior should not change.

And fifth, have fun! Enjoy the time you spend with your animal companion. Keep in mind that once they learn what you're trying to teach them, you will both have a more fulfilling relationship.

Chapter 6

MARK HARDEN

(LOS ANGELES COUNTY, CALIFORNIA)

Chico at home

Chico as Hachi in *Hachi: A Dog's Tale*
Forever Faithful

Mark Harden

How do you train a dog to play the lead in a major motion picture when he's just not that into you... or treats, or praise, or affection? I was about to get schooled by an Akita named Chico — the most challenging dog I have ever trained.

Frequently, a script calls for a unique or specific breed to play a part. In those cases, adopting a shelter dog or finding the right dog from a breed rescue group is not an option. As movie animal trainers, we need to enlist a cooperative breeder who is willing to lease us a dog for the project and let us return him when it is finished. Even if we happened to find exactly the right dog for a role, odds are that such a unique and specific-looking animal would not get much future work. In that case, we'd find a good home for the dog after the project finished.

I had just finished shooting the third installment in the *Pirates of the Caribbean* series, *At World's End*, when my boss, Boone Narr, owner of Boone's Animals for Hollywood, and I drove from his ranch in northern Los Angeles County to Anaheim. We were meeting a caring and respected Japanese Akita breeder, Debra Anibal, in a hotel parking lot near Disneyland. Debra was bringing us two of her Akitas, Chico and Layla. She had agreed to let us borrow the dogs to play the part of Hachi in the film *Hachi: A Dog's Tale*. Later, Debra helped us complete our team by introducing us to Forrest, a four-year-old Akita who lived in New Jersey.

Not Mine to Keep

Whichever way I find the best dogs for a role, I spend several intense months working with them and then have to say good-bye, possibly forever. Because the dogs I work with don't belong to me, and I know I won't be keeping them, I defensively create a protective wall. I try to establish a close and fun, yet professional, relationship, much like a teacher who knows that in nine months his students will move on to the next class.

I had no experience with Akitas. Folklore about the breed was positive, though. The Japanese originally bred the dogs to hunt. Considered national treasures, they serve as symbols of longevity, health, and happiness. Parents of newborns receive Akita statues as gifts representing wishes for the baby to have a long and happy life.

Before I met Debra in Anaheim, she had cautioned me that Japanese Akitas are smart though stubborn; they are aloof and difficult to train. She said I could teach the dogs tricks but wished me luck in getting them to do those tricks repetitively, when and where I wanted. "You'll never see an Akita in the agility ring," she had said.

Still, I felt excited to be meeting a new animal, especially a breed I'd never worked with before. After we exchanged a few pleasantries, Debra opened her truck's camper shell. She unlatched one of the crates, quickly slipped a leash on Chico, handed him over, and instructed me to take him to the lawn. I walked him to some bushes and let the dog do his business. Chico and I never had so much as a sniff or a pet before we headed back to Debra and his sister, Layla.

"He likes you," Debra said.

"Really?" I asked. "It doesn't even seem like he knows I exist."

Trust Me, Chico

Regardless of Chico's aloofness, my job was to turn him into the loyal and loving Hachi. The movie, an Americanized film based on a true Japanese story from the 1920s, tells of a faithful Akita named Hachiko who accompanied his master, Parker Wilson (Richard Gere), to the train station every morning and met him there every evening when Parker returned from work. (*Spoiler alert!*) One day, Parker died at work and never returned home. Hachi waited for Parker, dutifully returning every evening until the dog's own death, nine years later.

I've read a hundred scripts in my career, and few, if any, have moved me to tears. After I reviewed the script for *Hachi: A Dog's Tale*, I looked through blurry eyes at this gorgeous, standoffish dog who had come into my life for the film. *Hachi*'s screenwriter had written the breed's distance and lack of desire to please into the script. But I found it difficult to imagine Chico having for me...or anybody...the love and loyalty Hachi had felt for Parker.

Chico barely looked at me for the first month. He wouldn't eat out of my hand or even in my presence. I'd put his food bowl in front of him, and he wouldn't touch it. I'd walk away and come back twenty minutes later to find the bowl empty.

Akitas are not innately mean dogs. But they don't run up to every stranger, eager to play fetch. Although Chico would never turn into a friendly dog, before I could get him to perform on set, I had to help him become comfortable around people he didn't know.

A film set is a harried, odd, ever-changing environment with a hundred or more bustling people doing specific jobs. Early in our training, Chico hadn't shown any anxiety around strange equipment. Strange people were another matter.

In my line of work, trust is the most important thing. The relationship between a trainer and animal is like that between a superhero and a skeptical leading lady. He extends his hand and says, "Trust me." She takes his hand, and together they fly.

In order to gain Chico's trust, I had to get into his head. I needed to find some way to motivate this dog with something he would enjoy and to let him know when I was pleased with him. I also had to persuade him to care about pleasing me. Fortunately, I had been training animals for a total of over thirty years, including eighteen years working on set with a variety of wild animals, all with their own peculiarities.

Life before Chico

I grew up in a small Northern California lumber town in a family with pets, although we wouldn't have been considered "animal people." After spending my seventh-grade summer watching *Flipper* reruns, I wanted to work with dolphins. I quietly held on to this dream until my sophomore year in college, when I moved to Southern California to study in the Exotic Animal Training and Management Program at Moorpark College. Before I graduated, Animal Actors of Hollywood, a premier wild animal–training facility in Thousand Oaks, California, recruited me to work with sea lions in a Hawaiian circus. Then the sea lions got cast in a TV pilot called *Catalina Sea Lab*, and I spent an incredible month with them, working on the beach and in the ocean. Though they weren't dolphins, the experience with sea lions convinced me that I'd found my calling as an animal trainer.

In spite of having no previous exposure to them, training wolves, primates, birds, and sea lions came easily to me. But I lacked a natural sense for big cats. For the entire eighteen years I worked with them, I learned to control my fear but remained afraid of cats. Unbelievably, there came a time when I was considered the go-to leopard guy.

The best career advice I got (which I ignored) came from a crusty old-timer who told me, "If you really want to be happy, find another line of work." Working with animals is a 24/7 job that falls more in line with the old adage "Find something you love that you'd do for free, then find a way to get paid."

Though my career started with a bang, while hoping for my next big break, I spent the next several years earning $125 per week for cleaning and feeding at a facility that housed exotic animals. I knew then that if I really wanted this career, I'd need to learn everything I could and make myself indispensable.

While working with a large variety of animals and watching a diverse group of experienced trainers, I gradually developed my own creative training style. I learned what made animals similar and how individuals of the same species could differ. I discovered how a monkey might be trained like a bird and a lion trained more like a wolf than a tiger.

Adjusting to Chico

When Chico failed to respond to my normal dog-training techniques, with my previous experience adjusting to animals' individual needs, I was prepared to change my approach. Instead of teaching him traditional movie tricks — sit, stay, on your feet, speak, etc. — I decided to start him on an agility course. Agility tricks are tangible; they make sense to a dog. See a hurdle and jump it; see a tunnel and go through it; see the A-frame and go over it. As with training a chicken to play the piano, the prop becomes the animal's cue for a specific action. Since nothing I had offered so far interested him, I hoped the agility tricks might become self-rewarding. My goal was not to teach Chico agility; it was to teach him to learn.

Starting simply, I asked Chico to hop onto a table and helped him up to it. When he did the action, I offered a treat, told him he was good, and scratched behind his ears. At first, he refused the treat and barely tolerated my praise and affection, but I repeated the action until he voluntarily hopped onto the table. Then I set up a low agility hurdle and let him run ahead of me while leading him over it. After he leaped over the hurdle, he proudly jumped onto the table. Eureka! The table had become his reward.

I added a plank walk to Chico's agility course. Each new prop became an obstacle between him and his reward (the table). Every time I added a new obstacle, he'd flatten his ears and let his tail droop. (Normally held

Chico and Mark

up in a tight coil against the dog's back, an Akita's tail is a reliable barometer to the animal's mood.) Each time he did a trick with an agility prop and ultimately reached the table, his ears perked up, and his tail tightened.

One day, after I had introduced Chico to all the props in a circular order, I started him at the beginning and let him go. He sprinted through the course, finishing proudly by standing on the table. This time, he took the treat and actually seemed to enjoy my praise and affection.

I had broken the code and unlocked his potential. From that day forward, Chico learned his movie tricks with ease. He understood the process. What had once seemed random now made sense to him. Not only did he work; he liked it. We became a team.

Often, dogs who are easy to train try to get one step ahead of their trainer. They anticipate the next trick or skip a few tricks in the middle of a series to get the reward quicker. I call them "cheaters." Not Chico. He became one of the most honest dogs I've ever worked with. I could place him on his mark and walk two hundred feet back to the camera. Patiently, he would wait until I gave him his cue, even when he knew what the trick would be. Through our atypical training process, he had learned to trust that I would tell him what to do next.

"Acting" Animals

Animals don't *really* act. If a dog is supposed to have a sad moment in a movie, I can't go all Stanislavski (method acting) and ask him to recall a miserable moment from his past, because animals live in the present. When I encounter a scene in a script that requires an emotion like sadness, I ask myself what physical behaviors this animal can do to elicit that feeling in humans. Then I teach the behavior, put it on cue, and call it a trick.

I might even teach a few "microtricks" to further sell the emotion. For example, I will teach a sequence like this: mark (a spot to stand on), come/mark (go to the spot), easy (move slowly), easy, come/mark, and head down (lower your head while walking, standing, sitting, or lying down). Add violins and some mood lighting, and to an audience, the dog looks sad. The same series of tricks can also be used to convey apathy, lethargy, or guilt.

The character Hachi not only shows a range of human emotions but also goes through a complete life cycle, from puppyhood to death. We needed to form a team of dogs to portray Hachi at different stages of his life. Since red-and-white Akitas are fairly rare and would grow too quickly over the duration of shooting a movie, we cast a small Japanese breed, the Shiba Inu, to play Hachi as a puppy. In Rhode Island, where the movie was filmed, a local dog trainer trained the puppies for us. We also needed to represent a young-adult Hachi prior to Parker's death, an adult Hachi after Parker's death, and an old, dying Hachi.

Chico, Layla, and Forrest, plus the Shiba Inu puppies, created the arc of Hachi's character. We carefully cast the dogs according to their personalities and inserted them into the movie at the right moment for maximum impact. Two-year-old Chico and Layla played the young-adult and adult Hachi. Four-year-old Forrest played the old, dying dog.

Chico's sister, Layla, is the un-Akita. She acts like a golden retriever — she loves everybody, greets strangers like long-lost friends, and lavishes kisses on anybody. We used her mostly with Richard Gere, early in the film, to show Parker and Hachi bonding and Hachi's love and devotion. In the early part of the movie, Chico did many of the physical shots, such as jumping over or digging under the fence to get out. After Parker's death, when Hachi waits for Parker at the train station while ignoring passersby, that, too, is Chico.

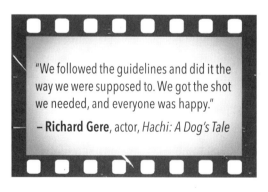

"We followed the guidelines and did it the way we were supposed to. We got the shot we needed, and everyone was happy."

– **Richard Gere**, actor, *Hachi: A Dog's Tale*

To create the emotion of expectation for Hachi at the train station, I put Chico on his "waiting" mark outside the depot. As the camera rolled, I slipped into the station house, and the camera operators filmed Chico looking for me. Then extras streamed out the station doors, and Chico looked at each one, expecting me to be among them. When they called cut, I came running out and told Chico what a good boy he was. After Parker (Richard Gere) came out of the train station, friendly Layla charged over to greet him.

Once Parker dies in the film, Hachi is supposed to have changed. He moves through the town, ignoring everybody. He stays at the station, oblivious, staring at the doors, waiting for Parker to return. Of course, Parker never again comes home on the train, so Hachi stoically trots back to where he's been living. Because Chico truly didn't care whether or not the other characters or extras petted or fed him, Chico's aloof nature was perfect for selling those scenes.

In the scene that showed Parker's family coming to the depot to take Hachi home, the dog looks reluctant to go. They have to put a leash on him and pull him away. No acting required. Chico reluctantly went with the family because I told him to let them take him. He would rather have stayed with me. Layla would have given the family a big kiss, jumped in their car, and said, "Let's go."

Old Hachi

Getting the opportunity to create an old Hachi drew me to this project. I figured the challenge of training a young dog to convincingly play an old dog on the big screen would utilize everything I'd learned and require all my self-discipline. I am an energetic, some might say hyperkinetic, trainer. I use my entire being — my highs, lows, voice, and energy — to draw a performance out of my animals. To train Forrest to act old when he was a spunky four-year-old, I'd have to rein in my natural energy. I'd teach him the right tricks in the right order and work with him as if he were actually an old dog.

The movie's original director, however, had other plans. He wanted us to cast a very old dog to play old Hachi. Not only did this quash my enthusiasm; it put me in the awkward position of refusing a director's request. Boone and I agreed — we would not do it. By the time a dog physically *appears* old on screen, he's too elderly to be put through the rigors of training for the work. It would not be good for the dog or the project. Fortunately, a change of filming schedule led to a change of leadership, and Lasse Hallström took the helm as director. He understood why we couldn't use a senior dog and trusted us to teach Forrest to act old.

The first thing that struck me upon meeting Forrest was that he was definitely not an old dog. With a playful though awkward disposition, Forrest was a bit goofy in a lovable way. He had a beautifully large head and was marked exactly like Chico and Layla. Because of his perpetual playfulness, I had to suck in all my energy while training him to act old. I imagined how I wanted to work with Forrest on set. Visualizing the desired results made planning easier. It also prevented me from falling back on my old ways of training dogs.

We rehearsed by my showing Forrest a pattern and letting him do the scene without coaching or cues. To make his movements slow and deliberate, I taught him "easy." When he was supposed to lie down, I had Forrest first walk in a slow circle, then lie down. Instead of teaching Forrest to go to a mark the traditional way, I taught him to put one foot on a small, fifty-cent-piece-sized mark. I then lined up dozens of the small marks, asking him to step on them one at a time and alternate left and right paws, as if he was walking on stepping-stones. Not only did this movement slow his gait, but it also had the added benefit of encouraging him to keep his head down while watching his feet.

Adding the Marks of Aging

Now that he was starting to *act* old, I needed to figure out how to make Forrest *look* old. I knew the production company would have a makeup artist on set who could do the job of aging Forrest for the camera, but Boone and I didn't want to wait. Before convincing the producers and Lasse that we could accomplish the physical appearance of old Hachi, we had to prove it to ourselves.

I personally created and applied Forrest's old-age makeup. I used groomer's chalk, a commercially available product that covers slight flaws on show dogs. The chalk added color and grit and dulled the dog's coat. I also used nontoxic human makeup and hair products, like pomade and styling mayonnaise, to change Forrest's hair texture and help keep the chalk in place. Mascara created the fly-bitten look around his ears, and eyeliner mimicked the red tear and toe-lick stains often found on older dogs. I used an elastic band to attach a small fishing weight to Forrest's tail to keep it down while he walked.

Anxious to put the look all together, we took our old Hachi to a park near Boone's ranch. By that time, I needed to use only three marks — one at the start of the walk, a second at the corner or middle, and a third at the end. Forrest would walk the width of the park to a corner (about 75 feet), stop, turn right, and continue walking the length of the area (about 150 feet). Another trainer videotaped the action. I quietly told Forrest to go. As I had practiced, although it was difficult for me, I didn't say another word until the dog reached his end mark, one minute and thirty-five seconds later. When we replayed the tape, we were glad to see that Forrest convincingly looked like a tired old dog walking a familiar path he'd traveled a thousand times. We sent the video to Lasse to assure him that he had a very old Hachi to film.

Old Hachi On Set

After we were on the set in Woonsocket, Rhode Island, I made it clear to the assistant director that I wouldn't run to bring Forrest to the set. Not wanting to seem like a prima donna trainer, I explained that I'd rather wait with Forrest on set for twenty minutes than feel rushed and anxious to bring him there for his scenes. I needed to maintain low energy so as to tamp down the dog's excitement.

The crew saw Forrest for the first time as he and I slowly ambled toward them. In that moment, they understood what we had accomplished. A respectful hush settled over the set.

Though *Hachi: A Dog's Tale* never played in U.S. theaters, it did very well on DVD and had a successful international theatrical run. I've watched it with many people. I enjoy the audible gasp from first-time viewers during the moment Forrest, as old Hachi, makes his entrance. He trudges up the snowy street, trips as he mounts the train depot stairs, and finally climbs up onto his waiting place. I feel a sense of pride and accomplishment while watching how the elements of those scenes — the training, makeup, sets, and directed action — all come together to elicit a collective and compassionate sigh from audiences the world over.

Chico Today

Originally, we leased Chico from Debra with every intention of returning him. By the end of filming, I started regretting that plan. He and I had been through a lot together. Chico had grown into such a wonderful and confident dog, and I had learned so much from him.

During our prep time, I'd rolled scenes in my mind until we got them right. I'd mentally practiced a speech to Richard Gere about the pitfalls of meeting an Akita for the first time and how coming on too strong could sour their relationship forever. Yet not once did I imagine giving Chico back to Debra. And now, I didn't want to let him go.

Debra frequently visited us while we prepared Chico and Layla, and delighted at watching them work for us so happily. When we returned with Chico and Layla to California from Rhode Island, Debra came out to the ranch to greet them. She stood by the fence of the agility yard while Chico and I romped. Later, as we both stroked Chico's perfect coat, Debra said, "You know you have to keep him, right? Akitas don't bond easily, and he's so bound to you. That won't happen again. I want you to have him."

Mark, Chico, and Lori

What?!

Chico now lives with me. He's more than a family pet; he's a family member, a companion, and a friend. He enjoys coming to work with me or staying home and keeping my wife, Lori, company. On the days he stays home, I am told, he dutifully marches up the stairs moments before five o'clock. Like Hachi, he sits in our bay window and waits for me. My wife, half jokingly, warns me not to die at work. She can't even drive my car when I'm away on location, because it's difficult for her to watch the disappointment on Chico's face when he realizes it's she, not I, who has pulled into the driveway.

Hachi: A Dog's Tale was one of the best moviemaking experiences of my career, and I will pass down memories of it to my grandchildren. Chico will always be the dog who made me appreciate the leap I've asked countless animals to take into this zany world of movies. Most dogs just jump into the experience. Chico let me take nothing for granted. He made me prove myself worthy, and only then did he trust that, together, we could fly.

Tips for Training Dogs from Mark Harden

Before teaching a trick to your dog, have a clear picture in your mind of what you want it to look like. If your dog is like Chico, you might have to start a long way from the end and shape the trick through a series of tiny steps. If you keep an image of the result in your mind, you won't easily get lost along the way.

Dogs are not all motivated by the same things. Find what inspires your dog, whether it's food, toys, roughhousing, or quiet petting. Mix up motivators to keep your dog on his toes and on your team while you build a repertoire of fun and useful behaviors.

Don't try to be something you are not. You are not a wolf, a chew toy, or a drill sergeant. When working with your dog, simply be your best self.

Guido as Paulie in *Paulie*
The Sky's the Limit

Mark Harden

How do you stay ahead of a bird who learns tricks faster than you can teach them? I was about to find out when I met Guido, the blue-crowned conure who played the title role in the movie *Paulie*.

In *Paulie*, Tony Shalhoub plays Misha. He happens upon Paulie, played by Guido and voiced by Jay Mohr, living in the basement of an animal research lab where Misha is a janitor. Misha discovers, to his amazement, that this discarded bird not only talks but converses. By promising to help Paulie find his way home, Misha persuades him to share his dramatic life story.

The director, John Roberts, and the producers chose blue-crowned conures to play Paulie and picked another group of conures (Jendays,

Movie poster for *Paulie*

Nandays, and cherry heads) to play the other bird characters Paulie encounters on his journey. They also chose Boone's Animals for Hollywood to cast and train the birds. Boone invited me to train the lead bird.

Because Paulie appeared in nearly every scene and had numerous flying shots, we needed multiple birds for the part. I trained four. Most of them came from breeding facilities and had full flight feathers. Guido, a younger bird, came with clipped wings. Properly clipping a pet bird's feathers doesn't hurt them. It's like cutting hair and could possibly save the bird's life. Those feathers, however, do not grow back like hair. New feathers replace them during a molt, and that can take many months.

I'd like to take credit for picking Guido to play the lead, but I can't. I won a game of blue-crown roulette. Three of my birds — Faith, Zip, and Mango — had full flight ability, and Guido didn't. By default, they became fliers, and Guido became what I call a "tabletop" bird.

The fliers would need to get fit and learn to fly in a wind machine, fly to me, and follow me in a moving vehicle. They would have to fly in big circles in the sky — at first on a safety line and then free. Guido would need to learn *everything* for the movie that didn't involve flying. We began with me on a stool and him on the top of a table.

Nothing I do in my work beats flying birds. I have flown thousands of them, from tiny finches to majestic eagles. I never tire of it. Sometimes, when I have a break, I'll take a flock of pigeons and train them to fly to me just for fun.

Tabletop training, on the other hand, is physically tedious and mentally exhausting. It always starts the same. Me starring blankly, wondering where to begin, like Michelangelo waiting for a block of marble to reveal its masterpiece. Hopefully, it ends with a Guido — my *David*. I get distracted just thinking about it.

Training Guido and the Other Birds

To train a bird, I have to teach the bird to recognize the sound of a clicker. I pair the clicker with a food reward. I try to use as much maintenance food (prepared pellets and veggies) as possible, to ensure the bird is getting a proper diet. I add special treats (fruit, safflower seeds, sunflower seeds) to keep his interest. Eventually, he'll equate the click with food — like an IOU. Then I can string many behaviors together, clicking to let him know he's on the right track and will get a big payday at the end.

Boone contacted me to work on *Paulie* while I was finishing another film. Wanting to get a head start, I brought Guido and Faith home and took them to the set where I was working every day. We got to know each other a bit. First, I needed to teach Guido some tricks, so I started clicker-training him and getting Faith to take those first short flights from perch to hand.

When I arrived for my first day of training at Boone's compound, the other trainers came out to greet me and meet Faith and Guido. Though Boone had assembled a great team of trainers for the *Paulie* birds, few had much bird-training experience. I like training trainers almost as much as I like training animals, so I was glad to bring my experience to the party. I confidently opened the back of my car. With safety line in my right hand, I opened Faith's cage. As I reached in to have her step up on my left hand, she flew right by me. Boom. Like that, she was gone.

Humility may be the most important tool in a trainer's toolbox. It keeps you honest and cautious. Fortunately, Faith didn't fly far. I retrieved her, put the line on her, and reminded everyone what I had said at a prior meeting: "You can't really say you fly birds until you've lost one." I remember an old-timer telling me you can learn *something* from everybody. If you think not, you've stopped learning. There I was, prepared to teach others, and still I had so much to learn, with those little blue-headed birds as my teachers.

Making Progress

We prepped for four months. The fliers grew stronger every day, though I worried about their small size. Regardless of their strength and training, it seemed the slightest breeze might blow them off course, and they'd be gone. Guido also progressed daily, eagerly learning everything I taught. I read the script and composed a daunting list of the written tricks required. I analyzed the script again and made another list of the tricks implied

Mark Harden at the Grand Canyon teaching flying birds for *Paulie*

but unwritten: flap your wings; bob your head; raise your right wing; raise the other wing; give me your right foot; give me your left foot; back up; on your mark; look left; look right. In addition, Guido learned to lie down like a dog and fall backward off his perch. Though the computer team would move his beak in postproduction, I thought teaching him head and beak movements would help sell the dialogue.

I knew from experience that Guido would have to perform these tricks looking at actors, not at me. With dogs, we teach a "look away" so the camera can get shots from behind the dog. We try to teach a few simple "look away" tricks, like "lie down away" and "sit away," but a dog's desire to keep eye contact with his trainer can make it difficult. Once I started teaching Guido "away," I realized his peripheral vision was so wide that he could see me almost everywhere I stood. However, he quickly caught on to the "look away" command and learned to do most of his behaviors without facing me.

Training at the ranch and working on a set are very different things. You never know what might upset or distract an inexperienced animal. During our prep period, we try to re-create the on-set experience as well as we can. We play music with sound effects, hang lights and umbrellas, have fake cameras and boom mics, drag cables, and do anything that might help prepare the animals for the craziness of a movie set. No matter what we do, the first week on set is full of surprises.

For *Paulie*, we had the luxury of testing the birds on camera a few weeks before principal photography started. Production wanted to do some film or screen tests with Tony Shalhoub and the birds. At this point in the story, Paulie is supposed to perform almost entirely in his cage. It might seem as if cage performances would be easy because the bird can't fly away. However, the trainer can't access the bird in a cage. There is a forest of flags, light stands, and other obstacles between the trainers and our little animal actors, so it makes cage work challenging.

Of course, we practiced during our prep period. But the ways we needed to improve Guido's training became apparent during these pre-shoot days. We hadn't anticipated Guido's reaction to having a stranger (Tony) pick up and carry the cage around and how his actions would cause Guido to start "acting." We had to figure out how to reset Guido at the end of each take without opening his cage door, since we couldn't get to him while the scene was in progress. What a wake-up call. We had all the pieces; we just weren't ready to put the puzzle together. Fortunately, we still had time to address the problems.

I don't remember anything specifically going wrong after the first week of filming, so I'll assume it went reasonably well. I do remember when I discovered what a special animal Guido was. We were shooting the doctor's office scene at night, a few weeks into filming. Paulie was to be sleeping in his cage, when the doctor enters. Paulie fakes sleep, over-hearing the doctor plotting on the phone. Prepared for this scene, I taught Guido to "sleep" by training him to turn his head around and nestle his beak into his back — the way a parrot sleeps. That morning, the director asked what Guido looked like when he slept. I proudly showed him our trick. He hated it. He said it looked like a headless bird and asked if Guido could sleep another way.

Seriously? We were shooting the scene that evening.

I started training the new trick right away and chained a few old tricks together to build it. I asked Guido to lift his wing and turn his head. I held a treat under his wing where I wanted his head to land. Then I clicked the clicker and gave him the treat. He got it. After a few tries, Guido knew what I wanted. I added the cue "Night, night," and we practiced between scenes all day. By the time they set up for the doctor's office scene, we were ready. That night, I knew I had a teammate — one who was always on my side, eager to learn, and happy to perform.

Guido expanded my concept of training. He taught me to abandon preconceived notions and that only my creativity and imagination limited what I could train and what he could learn.

Excess Baggage

All animals (including humans) carry physical and psychological baggage; some are species specific and others particular to the individual. As an animal trainer, I must learn as much as I can about the animal I'm working with: their eating and sleeping habits, social structure, and learning style. I even want to know how the animal's mother might raise her young. The more I know, the healthier and happier I can keep the animals and the quicker I can tell when something is wrong.

Parrots like Guido are especially tricky. Maintaining their feather health becomes an obsession. While working with the blue-and-gold macaws, Chip and Salsa, on the *Pirates of the Caribbean* films (three movies shot over a three-year period), I worried incessantly. I imagined waking up and finding Salsa had broken his gorgeous three-and-a-half-foot-long tail feathers or Chip had become a plucker. Because parrots are intelligent, inquisitive, mischievous creatures of habit, maintaining their mental health becomes challenging, too. Their nature provides both funny and embarrassing moments on set.

Occasionally, Salsa would get bored with sitting on the pirate Cotton's shoulder all day and yell, "Cut!" in the middle of a scene. Everybody would stop acting. The director would jump out of his chair, yelling, "Who said that?" as a boat full of pirates and crew turned toward the bird.

Parrots also have an innate need to roost together at night. It makes sense in the wild, since there is security in numbers. They accomplish this by screeching at the top of their lungs, just before sunset, so all the birds from miles away know what tree everybody's sleeping in that night. All well and good in the wild, but on a movie set, it's earsplitting, annoying, and embarrassing.

Another aspect of a parrot's nature also creates challenges. Parrots, being extremely social, arrive on a set, like other social animals, looking to make meaningful connections and establish their position on the social ladder. In short, they are opinionated and judgmental. All my best training efforts can go out the window the moment my bird decides to hate or love somebody on the set. If I fail to communicate to both the animal and the crew how socially neutral this environment must be, I fail the job.

The blue-and-gold macaws persisted in their desire to judge throughout the long shooting schedule. Though they performed well, they kept me on my toes. Fortunately, Guido did not share the macaws' need for social approval. He and I connected on a much deeper level. He came to work every day as a professional, leaving his excess baggage at home and asking only, "What are we doing today, boss?"

Guido Today

We kept Guido and three other blue-crowned conures from *Paulie* and found caring homes for the others. Guido still loves to work and frequently gets small parts in commercials, movies, or TV shows. Every time I take him out to work, I can't believe how much that tiny brain remembers. I usually ask him to show me what he knows, since I've forgotten.

He seems to understand that when we are out in my world, I am the boss. However, in his world, living with *his girls*, he rules the roost. When I go to visit him, the females attack me. He bobs his head, egging them on, as if to say, "Yeah, that's right." The other trainers at Boone's get a chuckle, seeing me emerge bloodied from Guido's cage. But once we get back to work, he's still the sweet, smart, eager star of *Paulie*, able to recall any of his over one hundred tricks and ready to learn more. I am again humbled by this little blue-headed parrot who reminds me never to stop learning.

Guido now

Tips for Training Parrots
from Mark Harden

Provide plenty of stimulation for your pet parrot in the form of destructible toys. Hide his special food treats in things he can pull apart, open, or destroy, to engage his very active brain and simulate his foraging instincts.

As heartwarming as it is to be the object of your bird's affection, remember that parrots tend to mate for life, often to the exclusion of others. You are not his mate and must teach him that lashing out at others is unacceptable.

Parrots live long lives. Make a plan for the placement of your bird should he outlive you. Keep in mind that a happy, well-balanced, well-socialized pet is easy to place. A cranky, aggressive, grieving biter isn't.

Buy a parrot-training book, a clicker, and special treats, and start teaching tricks to your bird. They love it; you'll love it. The sky's the limit.

Oscar as Butch in
Cats & Dogs: The Revenge of Kitty Galore
The Right Dog for the Job

Mark Harden

I often joke with crew members on set when they comment
on how well my dogs behave while complaining about their own. I tell
them not to be deceived — this dog's not really a pet; he just plays one on
TV. Though I'm just having a little fun, twisting an old Hollywood story
about an actor who plays a doctor on a TV series and gets asked for medical advice in a restaurant, I'm only half joking. In over thirty years of
training animals for film, I've discovered that failed pets generally make
the best actors.

Like human performers, animal actors need larger-than-life personalities. When I go to a shelter or visit a breed rescue, I look for those

Mark Harden
and Oscar

"Charlie Sheen" types who consider themselves winners because they think their bad behavior (barking when they want, chewing what they want, biting who they want) brought them attention. "Winning" is probably what landed them in the pound. In the real world, these pets' exhausted owners try to train their dogs *not* to do things. In my world, I get to train the dogs *to* do things. When I put their misbehaviors on cue and their "winning" attitude to work, everybody wins.

When Larry Guterman, director of the movie *Cats & Dogs*, picked Anatolian shepherds to play Butch in the movie, I contacted Anatolian Shepherd Rescue to help me find the right dog. Responsible breeders of purebred dogs organize rescue efforts to keep their breed out of shelters and in suitable homes. Anatolian shepherds are a rare breed and perhaps the world's best large, powerful livestock guardians. They are used in South Africa and Zimbabwe to protect flocks against leopards and cheetahs. Anatolians are bred to be suspicious and territorial, which often makes them less-than-ideal pets.

Anatolian Shepherd Rescue helped me launch a nationwide search and find Noah, my first Anatolian. At that time, one-year-old Noah had outgrown his living situation and, at 135 pounds, had succeeded at doing everything his way — "winning"! The woman who raised him realized this situation was untenable. Because of his size and strength, she feared Noah might become dangerous. She listed him on the breed-rescue website but committed to keeping him until they found a new home. When I saw Noah's photo and heard his story, I knew he was the dog for me. Anatolian Shepherd Rescue helped me arrange his flight from Albany, New York, to Los Angeles. The rest, as they say, is Hollywood history. Noah trained up beautifully and made a perfect Butch for *Cats & Dogs*.

Oscar and Emmy

Ten years later, Warner Bros. Pictures decided to make a sequel to *Cats & Dogs*. Butch would again play a pivotal and heroic role. In the sequel, *Cats & Dogs: The Revenge of Kitty Galore*, the vengeful ex-MEOWS agent Kitty Galore plots to make cats rulers of the world, turning dogs into their slaves. At the DOG spy agency, Lou (the beagle from the first film) contacts Butch (now a world-weary veteran spy) to thwart their plan. Lou recruits help from Diggs, a German shepherd and overly zealous but failed San Francisco police dog. Butch must spring Diggs from the pound and tame his bad instincts while grappling with his own bigotry toward cats — including Catherine, a MEOWS agent assigned to work with them.

Sadly, Noah had died of a heart attack a few years before the second movie. Once again, I enlisted the Anatolian Shepherd Rescue to help me fill the role of Butch. This time, they found a dog much closer to home. Oscar lived with an elderly couple in Northern California, on a ranch with five other Anatolians. Together, they protected the couple's herd of miniature horses.

Since Oscar lived in the Sierra Nevada, only a six-hour drive away, I made an appointment to meet him in person — a luxury I hadn't had with Noah. Skeptically following my GPS, a new technology at the time, I drove to Sacramento. As instructed, I cut east into the foothills. Having grown up in the Sierras, I know how beautiful they are on the worst of days. On this particularly gray and misty morning, they were magical. I wound my way through the hills, seemingly forever, starting to doubt this chatty map-in-a-box. I crested a ridge with the GPS voice telling me that my destination was near. The sun, breaking through the low clouds, bathed in golden light an idyllic farmhouse that was surrounded by green meadows and California oaks. As I drove up the driveway, the scene became more surreal. It seemed I'd slipped down a rabbit hole, like Alice from *Alice in Wonderland*. The dogs I saw in this field were bigger than the horses.

Oscar's owners met me at the gate of their ranch, holding their dog on a leash. All huge and gangly, he wagged his whole body from head to tail. Did I mention he was huge? Not only the biggest Anatolian shepherd I had ever met, Oscar was the biggest dog I had ever met. When he put his feet up on my shoulders, his chin rested on top of my head. He weighed 165 pounds.

At first glance, I knew I was taking Oscar, but I asked the owners why they wanted to get rid of him anyway. I can and do deal with a lot of dog misbehavior, but it's nice to know what I'm getting into. They explained their situation: They'd stopped breeding horses and were thinning the herd. They didn't need so many dogs. Besides, Oscar was more interested in what was going on up at their house than in the fields. Although he was a good-natured dog, they called Oscar the worst guardian they'd ever had. So he was the first to go.

Excuse me. Did I hear right? Further evidence I'd stepped through the looking glass. They wanted me to take this gorgeous dog because he wasn't mean or territorial enough, because he was just too sweet? I quickly agreed to "take him off their hands" and asked the man to help me get Oscar into the extra-large crate I had in my van. Though the dog hadn't been crated since he was a pup, he jumped right in. Anxious to leave before they changed their minds, I signed the papers and headed for the driver's door. The man noticed the other crate in my van and asked if I was looking for another dog. I explained my need to have multiple dogs to play the role of Butch and that I always carry an extra crate for luck.

I guess this was my lucky day. He introduced me to Emmy, Oscar's sister. Though smaller, Emmy was large for a female. She had Oscar's

Oscar (left) and
Emmy (right)

Mark Harden prepping Oscar in rocket for *Cats & Dogs: The Revenge of Kitty Galore*

shape and a smaller version of his head. She was a little shy but not freak-ishly afraid of strangers. "I'll take her," I said.

Emmy wasn't as eager to get into a crate as Oscar, so I decided to drive straight back to Boone's ranch. A bold choice with three hundred pounds of dog in my van. This wasn't to be the last time Emmy distin-guished herself from her brother.

Emmy made it through the movie. She was much more typically Anatolian than Oscar, taking umbrage at my assistant's attempts to tell her what to do. She learned the basics but never blossomed. Though she was a loving dog and nice to be around, I knew she'd rather be guarding a herd than understudying her little brother. When the movie finished filming in Vancouver, Canada, a local dog trainer on our team knew of a llama rancher looking for a guardian dog. We placed her there: the right dog for the job.

Noah, our original Butch, was a great working dog, possibly one of the best I've ever trained, but he was all Anatolian. He instinctively knew which animals and people were on the movie's team and which weren't. He worked happily beside any of the 112 dogs and cats assembled for the film. He never met a crew member he didn't love. However, all bets were off if an outsider breached *his* territory, even if that territory included a neighborhood *we* had invaded for the day and the outsider was a local schnauzer returning to his own home.

Oscar never had this problem. Uncharacteristic of the breed, he loved every dog, cat, creature, and crew member he met. He loved coming to work every day.

Oscar took to the training beautifully. He learned everything Noah had learned and more. He worked side by side with an experienced German shepherd named Rowdy and a persnickety Russian blue cat named Goose. One of his most difficult tricks, the retrieve, became his most useful. Anatolians aren't retrievers by nature, so I couldn't use, as a tool, an innate desire to pick things up and bring them to me. I couldn't rely on an obsession or a sense of fun as with another breed. I had to teach retrieving like a trick. I used that retrieve when he had to throw a stick; grab a cord to keep a bad cat from pulling him off a boat; look like he got his head stuck in an air-conditioning unit;

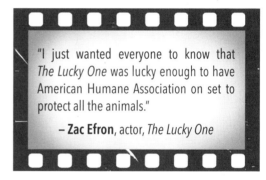

"I just wanted everyone to know that *The Lucky One* was lucky enough to have American Humane Association on set to protect all the animals."

– **Zac Efron**, actor, *The Lucky One*

open a parachute; and inflate a life raft. Often, when there were pages of dialogue, Oscar even had to hold a small black tennis ball in his mouth to keep his tongue from lolling out so the computer graphics team could make him talk.

Sometimes, the thing you'd least suspect causes you the most grief. Butch's first scene in the movie, when he heroically appears in Diggs's cell, required him to ride an elevator up through a hatch into the set above. He had to look ultraheroic, with his ears forward and eyes focused while entering through atmospheric smoke from the bottom of the frame.

During a computer-generated imagery (CGI) photo session, I learned that Oscar had never been off the ground. The CGI team came out to Boone's ranch in the early stages of their work, during our pre-training, to photograph the main characters against a gridded backdrop.

I jumped Oscar up onto a table they had set up about three feet off the ground. He started looking nervous. Fortunately, it was early in our prep, and I was able to train him through it. Knowing how important it was to have him comfortably ride the elevator in that shot, he and I rode up and down on a scissor lift every day we were in Vancouver until they shot the scene for the movie, and Oscar felt completely at ease.

Oscar Now

Oscar loves to work. He loves going to the set and hanging out in the training yard with the other dogs. However, dogs his size rarely get cast, and he was getting older and a bit less mobile. After a brief (but pivotal) role in *The Lucky One*, which starred Zac Efron, we decided to find Oscar a home. Someone who had previous experience with Anatolian shepherds adopted him. Oscar has adapted well to his new life as a house/office pet while enjoying the occasional day job and visit to the ranch. It doesn't get any better than that.

Tips for Training Large-Breed Dogs from Mark Harden

Large guardian dogs are bred with an elevated sense of suspicion and territory. It is critical to socialize these breeds early and often and continue exposing them to new things throughout their lives.

Establish social order early in a livestock guardian dog's life and work to maintain it throughout. Train and maintain obedience in your dog.

This is a working dog, so clearly define his job for him. Make sure he knows when and where to act on his natural inclinations toward suspicion, protection, and territoriality.

Chapter 7

JULES SYLVESTER
(THOUSAND OAKS, CALIFORNIA)

Kitty the Burmese python and Jules Sylvester

Kitty as the Burmese Python in *Snakes on a Plane*
How You Don't "Train" Snakes and Insects

Jules Sylvester

I love snakes. They are beautiful to me. I love to rescue snakes out of people's gardens, fridges, and rubbish piles. I've found them in the most amazing places. Snakes are escape artists. They disappear down somebody's toilet and are never seen again. After they have finished with snakes on a movie set, I want the crew to think of the experience as almost boring and even pleasant. They expect terrible things to happen. But instead, they've learned something.

I'm a person who has been able to turn a hobby into a career. For over forty-four years, I have been a professional snake wrangler and herpetologist. In 1980, I started my company, Reptile Rentals, Inc. For over 330 movies and countless commercials and television programs, we have supplied snakes, alligators, crocodiles, frogs, toads, crabs, lobsters, insects, lizards, mice, rats, scorpions, spiders, guinea pigs, rabbits, and turtles. The sign outside my office sardonically reads, "Trespassers will be poisoned."

Even though I'm sixty-one now, I still love my work. I'm the god-father of reptiles in this business. My handlers, male and female, and I have a spotless safety record of no bites, accidents, or problems. When asked how I do this work, I'm proud to say that I've never been bitten by a venomous snake. Getting bitten means you were doing something wrong. Using mechanical snake tongs, I work safely. If you don't have good tools for handling snakes, it's like defusing a land mine. I tell movie crews, "You shouldn't be surprised if a snake takes a shot at you. That's just something snakes do. When

> **DID YOU KNOW...?**
>
> By 1994, AHA's *Guidelines for the Safe Use of Animals in Filmed Media* had been revised several times. It now included specific standards for horses, birds, fish, snakes, and insects as well as transportation-to-set standards.

you go on a set, you know a snake will bite. But I don't know what the actor will do."

Kitty, the Snake Star

It was my pleasure to provide eighteen-foot Burmese python Kitty for her starring role in the movie *Snakes on a Plane*. Kitty could eat a large goat. I've seen pythons eat eighty-five-pound gazelles with horns. It takes two and a half weeks for them to digest their prey. Pythons are mottled brown, pale beige, and yellow, which gives them perfect camouflage for surviving in dry bush. You can be staring at what you believe is a giant pile of broken leaves, and it turns out to be a python.

Kitty was supposed to wrap around an actor and a Chihuahua and eat both of them. She was very gentle, as I draped her 250-pound body over an actor's shoulders and onto his lap. But the poor guy panicked and said, "I can't do this." I understood. Certain people have phobias. I don't judge them. We took the snake off the actor and used stunt doubles with rubber snakes so the guy wouldn't have a bloody heart attack. The movie used computer-generated imagery (CGI) when the snake swallowed the man from his head down.

The Snake Pit

I understood the actor's reluctance to get cozy with Kitty. He probably didn't have anything close to my unique background and experiences with snakes. I was born on the equator in Kenya, East Africa, and speak fluent Swahili. The boarding school where my parents sent me had no television and was surrounded by jungle. When I was fifteen, my family moved to Nairobi, and we lived about fifty feet away from Nairobi Snake Park near a snake pit. One day, I watched a sixteen-foot python cross the Nairobi River ravine. I told the staff at the snake park, and they said, "That must be Sonja." She had escaped about sixteen months earlier. A man dived over the bank of the ravine and landed on top of the python. He looked like Steve Irwin on steroids. The man stuffed the snake in a gunnysack, got on a motorcycle with her, and brought Sonja back home. Stunned into admiration, I declared, "I want that job."

The snake park hired me to cut grass in a pit where a thousand snakes lived. For over two years, I did the job on my hands and knees, using hand shears. Every time it looked as if a snake was going to attack me, I leaped six feet over the wall. I assumed all of the snakes were dangerous and wanted to kill me.

Jules Sylvester with sixteen-foot anaconda

After the snake-pit job, I wanted to learn everything imaginable about a variety of animal species. I worked as a taxidermist for a while and, later, as a lion keeper at the Edinburgh Zoo in Scotland. I caught four thousand venomous snakes for a safari company in Victoria Falls and served as curator for three years at the Zambezi Snake Park. Then I was drafted into the Rhodesian guerilla war (in what is now Zimbabwe), where I chased bad guys and caught venomous animals. Finally, in 1974,

I returned to my parents' farm in Kenya to find the TV series *Born Free* being filmed there. The production company hired me as a snake catcher and lion handler. That's when I met my mentor, Hubert Wells, chief animal trainer for *Out of Africa*, and I began working for Animal Actors of Hollywood.

"Training" and Caring for Snakes

As far as training goes, there is none with snakes. I consider myself to be in "reptile management." I'm a wrangler, not a trainer, for reptiles and bugs, because snakes and insects just don't listen. Insects don't learn anything from me. I have to figure out what they do naturally.

My fellow handler Marco Solis and I work in tandem to draw the snakes wherever they need to go for the shot. It's simply a matter of knowing the animals' instinctual habits to get them to move when and where I want. If a snake is rattling and everyone on set stays still, he will turn toward the moving camera to find someone to strike. It has nothing to do with me. Even though I say things such as "Marco, make him look at you," "Marco, move," it's not that the snake likes Marco better than me. The snake doesn't care anything about either of us.

At home, the snakes eat once a week. When we are on location, we may be gone for three weeks. We don't feed them when we are working, but wait until we go home, where they get fed a lot. Sometimes, they don't eat for a month, or up to three months. Then they eat again in the spring.

I did a television show called *Time Warp*. We needed a rattlesnake to rattle and pop a balloon. A Western diamondback snake was perfect for the part. They will always try to bite you. So we brought in four of them. We did the scene, and one snake rattled so hard that half of his rattle popped off. This is similar to shedding skin. It is no more painful for the snake than trimming a fingernail is for a person. When the rattle grows too long, it falls off. An irate woman called me after watching the episode and complained that the rattlesnake looked stressed when his tail fell off. I tried to explain snake physiology to her. She had lots of opinions but no knowledge. I said, "Nice to meet you. If you have any more questions, Google. Education is a wonderful thing."

Snake Safety

Before work with snakes begins on the set, I have a safety talk with the crew. "A snake has no sense of humor," I tell them. "If you piss him off, he will bite you. Snakes are very honest. They don't lie. Actors lie for a living. I haven't lost an actor yet."

I also explain that snakes hear fewer vibrations, so if a person screams in terror, the snake won't know it. I emphasize that no one should ever squeeze a snake. "Use a comfortable grip. Don't hurt my snakes. I will stop the scene if my snake is getting hurt." If I see that an actor can't handle the snake properly, I give him a rubber snake instead and say, "Squeeze away!"

On a movie set, if a producer wants one more take but the snake is done, I say, "It will take me two minutes to change this snake out." I like to add, "The snake is the priority here." Or I might turn to the American Humane Association (AHA) certified animal safety representative and ask, "Could you talk to that young man, please?" The AHA safety representatives are buffers. They take the heat and protect us from having the occasional producer or director try to force stuff that's bad for the animals. This kind of thing rarely happens to me because nobody hassles a guy with a rattlesnake. But the AHA safety representatives will step in for us if they have to.

To keep the snakes separated from the actors and crew, I put up barriers made of plywood sheets. A snake will always strike an object, so I have one person working the camera and another person protecting it. I tell everyone to be still while I place snakes back in their buckets.

My firm and absolute rule is: no practical jokes on the set. No running around with a rubber snake. I'm a control freak with my snakes on a set to make sure there are no bites or injuries. After all, the crew is entrusting me with their lives.

On each set, I make up names for the snakes, but not Apocalypse or anything that sounds like the end of the world. I want people to lose their fear of snakes and think of them almost like pets. So I call the girls Pom Pom or Foo Foo, and the guy snakes I name Chuck.

Oddly enough, after a while, the crew gets comfortable. The snakes are very gentle. They just want you to go away. Our job is to teach the crew to enjoy the animals and to be awed by their beauty. By the time they leave, they're enthralled and all say they want a snake for a pet. I say, "Your wife is going to shoot down that idea in a heartbeat."

Filming *Snakes on a Plane*

With all my years of handling snakes and teaching movie and television crews how to behave around them, providing escape-artist snakes for *Snakes on a Plane* had me working in my element. In the film, FBI agent Neville Flynn (Samuel L. Jackson) is transporting a witness who will testify against a mob boss. While flight attendant Claire Miller (Julianna Margulies) tries to keep her passengers safe on the flight from Honolulu to Los Angeles, Neville must battle a plane filled with venomous snakes.

For *Snakes on a Plane*, we supplied 500 snakes and drove 450 of them in a temperature-controlled van from California across the border into Canada. The other 50 came from Canadian snake handlers. We transported our snakes in twenty-two one-gallon plastic jars with holes drilled into them and packed in cooled chests.

The film used one-third live action, plus CGI, animatronics, and rubber snakes. Julianna Margulies was so afraid of snakes that she insisted that no snakes could be on the same stage or within two thousand feet of her. So we just didn't stay on the same stage with Julianna.

Samuel L. Jackson liked the snakes, but they weren't allowed on the set when he was there. His agents thought he might get bitten. Construction built a fifty-by-fifty-foot snake room on a set where the snakes could be fed, cleaned, and kept while not working. Common sense ruled the day, and Samuel often slipped into the snake room after a day of filming to check in on his costars.

We didn't use the 500 snakes at one time, but worked with four 75-member teams of identical snakes. It's my policy to never overwork the animals and to keep them stress-free. As the snakes got hot, tired, or grumpy, I rotated teams. Rather than movie doubles, we had quadruples for each team of snakes.

Tarantulas and Spiders, Too

In addition to snakes, I wrangle spiders, tadpoles, butterflies, and beetles for commercial clients, such as Subaru. We supply the maggots for dead-body scenes on the *CSI* series. Tarantulas are especially easy to work with because they crawl away from moving air. If I blow on a spider or tarantula's butt, it goes for cover. Insects are very predictable. If I want beetles to walk, I put them on a leaf, and they go underneath it. If the scene calls for an insect to be killed, I use fake bugs or ones that are already dead. Since insects only live for nine months, I have plenty of them.

Jules Sylvester with baboon spider

My motto is: "Everybody goes home alive. From fleas to elephants. There are no mortalities. Nothing is ever killed for entertainment." I count every insect or animal to make sure no one is left behind on the set. I use a tiny paintbrush to pick up stragglers.

Tips for Training Snakes
from Jules Sylvester

You don't actually train snakes. If you want them to move in a certain direction, you use their natural instincts. If they're out in the open, snakes naturally go from light to dark and look for cover from birds of prey.

If a snake naturally likes to climb, I put him on the floor, and he'll slither up to a higher spot. If a python is placed high, he wants to go down. Dropping or raising the temperature slows down or speeds up snakes and bugs.

Chapter 8

LARRY MADRID

(ACTON, CALIFORNIA)

Penguins in *Mr. Popper's Penguins*

Pinky and Richard Dent as the Penguins in
Mr. Popper's Penguins
Keeping It Cool

Larry Madrid

My associates Larry Payne, Scott Schweitzer, and Joe McCarter and I were the team responsible for training, in only a couple of weeks, eight gentoo penguins from the Montreal Biodome to do live action for *Mr. Popper's Penguins*. The gentoos, a species the producer had specifically requested, have their natural habitat in Antarctica. Red-orange beaks and feet the color of peaches make them stand out in an icy environment. Their white feather caps provide camouflage.

The penguins for this movie would need to waddle around the set, move on cue to and from scenes, and interact with Jim Carrey's character, Mr. Popper. In one scene, the penguins even sit on chairs at the dinner table. Computer-generated imagery (CGI) effects would show them dancing. But live, trained penguins were essential to making them look real, with accurate movements, bodies, and personalities.

The movie penguins had character names — Captain, Lovey, Bitey, Stinky, Loudy, and Nimrod. To identify them for their health records, our penguins were tagged on their flippers with elastic straps of different colored beads — orange, red, brown, yellow, purple and green, yellow and white, red and white, and black. We started referring to them by their colors. We named "Yellow" Richard Dent, after the Pro Football Hall of Fame player, because the bird had a small indentation (a dent) in his chest feathers. We named "Red and White" Pinky, and he was in many of the scenes. But for the most part, since the penguins all looked alike, they worked interchangeably.

Pinky was a penguin with a great personality, and everyone loved him. When penguins move together on land, they're called a "waddle," "colony," or "rookery." Pinky usually led his waddle when the penguins walked in a group. Between scenes, Pinky would often come over to us for fish, visit for a while, and flip his flippers in a friendly gesture. Wild penguins instinctively don't like people, but Pinky was sociable and not intimidated.

Pinky training for
Mr. Popper's Penguins

The stakes were as high as could be. Penguins were not only in the title of the film; they were its central characters. We had to get this right. We spent ten to twelve hours a day for seven days studying the penguins. We observed their tendencies, interacted with them, and tried to figure out where each one would best be suited for certain scenes and movements.

By the end of the first week, we were worried that we wouldn't have time to get the penguins to perform all the necessary actions. Not surprisingly, they were very standoffish. But movies are on a schedule, and so were we. When filming began, the penguins needed to be eating from us and not only feeding in their pool. After they accepted our food, the penguins had to eat on top of a wooden apple crate that we would use as their mark for film shots.

In spite of the number of bird species I'd trained — owls, eagles, parrots, canaries, starlings, quail, geese, waterfowl, ravens, crows, seagulls, vultures, pigeons, and macaws — I had never trained marine animals. It is always better to raise wild animals from infancy so that imprinting, or bonding, starts at a young age. This way, the animal depends on the trainer and becomes part of his family. The penguins in this movie were wild adult marine animals who had never been handled.

Drawing on Experience

The list of animal species I've trained for movies and television since becoming an animal trainer in 1976 seems endless, and I had to draw on my experience for the challenge of training penguins for *Mr. Popper's Penguins*. How did a young man who received a music scholarship at Pepperdine University wind up working with penguins and a wide range of animals while traveling to movie sets around the world?

During college, I worked at Magic Mountain Park in Southern California. By watching other animal trainers and gaining on-the-job education, I learned to train and care for lions, tigers, cougars, a bear, a leopard, and exotic hoof stock. I left Magic Mountain Park to work with camels and elephants at the San Diego Zoo. After I spent a couple of years out of the animal-training business, my uncle recommended me to Gary Gero, founder and president of Birds and Animals Unlimited. Gary gave me my big break when he hired me in 1984 to work at the Animal Show at Universal Studios. In my ten years there, I trained orangutans, chimps, birds of prey, small exotic animals, parrots, dogs, and cats. I interacted with a variety of species in front of thousands of people who came to thousands of our twenty-minute shows.

I was proud to be with a company that I believe pioneered many safety protocols and animal care standards for the motion picture industry, some of which are part of the safety guidelines American Humane

Association (AHA) promotes today. Because AHA representatives help to keep animals safe, I appreciate that they answer producers' questions when trainers with less experience than I need it. The AHA representatives also take notes that provide documentation of our work.

In 1992, I got the assignment to be a cat trainer on my first movie, *Hocus Pocus*, with Bette Midler, Sarah Jessica Parker, and Kathy Najimy. While filming and training the cat team for *Hocus Pocus*, I set a goal for myself: I wanted to compete with the best trainers in Hollywood and to be recognized as one of the best in this small community. I love animals, and now I knew that I enjoyed training them. Animals respond to and will work for people who love them. This motivated me to be as professional as possible, do the best job I could with movie animals, and learn how to train any animal.

Later in my career, I even worked with insects. In one movie, actor Sam Elliot was lying on his side. I had a cockroach run from below Sam's chin, under his nose, past his eye that was closest to the ground, past his forehead, and through his hair. The roach ended up in a little box I had placed outside the film shot.

Getting It Right

Not many people have a chance to work closely and interact intimately with Arctic penguins. Keepers at zoos don't spend a lot of time getting to know penguins. They go into their enclosures with a bucket of fish and feed the waddle. Penguins learn that they can trust the keepers as a food source, but the relationship is standoffish. Even to get penguins weighed, which involves moving them from one specific place to another and having them stand on a scale, takes months.

The penguins for our movie had to learn how to be weighed, accept fish as reward for behaviors, come to their marks on the set, and be comfortable around people. Penguins aren't like dogs, who are happy to see you and want to please humans. These wild penguins needed to understand that people would take care of and not hurt them and would be a nice source of food.

We found that if we threw down fish, the penguins would go for the food and eat it from us. I always use positive reinforcement for training. Since fish was the penguins' only motivation, sloppy, wet fish became my best friend. If we didn't have something to feed them, the penguins got bored and walked off. If we shook the fish bucket, which the penguins associated with food, the camera would get shots of them running toward a fish bucket out of camera range.

If we held our hands out flat in front of us, it was the penguins' signal to move away. Hand gestures allowed us to get them in or out of a shot without touching them or being in camera range. A flat broom, held in front of the penguins and twisted, got their attention. Subtly moving the broom in different directions caused them to stay or walk away. Sometimes, we held the penguins in a puppy pen that had walls covered with shade cloth for containment. When we opened the puppy pen door, the penguins darted into the shot. To get them out of the scene, we used the sound of a buzzer and rattled a bucket of food near the pen. After they were inside, we closed the door behind them.

Because of our patience and consistency, by the end of the second week, the penguins were getting to know and trust us. My team and I were able to get them to do specific behaviors with consistency. They were also learning to do patterns — a sequence of behaviors. An example of an A-to-B-to-C pattern behavior would be that the penguins entered a shot; went to and stayed with the actor; then came out of the shot when the trainers called them.

As a group, the penguins were brave and worked well together. As individuals, some needed each other to gain more confidence for interacting with the trainers. Others actually let us touch and even hold them. These more extroverted penguins were the ones we chose to do many of the camera close-ups and the film shots with only a penguin and an actor.

Jim Carrey, who played Mr. Popper, the main character, found the penguins interesting. He was willing to learn how to feed the penguins in a group, in which some were more aggressive than others, without dropping the fish. He hung out with them and was careful about their well-being.

Keeping It Cold

To simulate their natural environment, which needed to be very cold, we had the penguins live, and nest at night, in a freezer warehouse with a huge swimming pool and natural rocks. Their off-set living quarters were kept at thirty-six degrees. Their training area next to the housing was kept at forty-five degrees. Since it was too hard to maintain thirty-six to forty-five degrees all day on a huge soundstage, we acclimated the penguins to forty-five degrees in the training area and prepared them for being on set. They could work for short periods of time if the set heated to fifty degrees, but nothing above that temperature. The room where we held the penguins before they entered a scene and the truck that drove them to and from the set also had to be temperature controlled.

After filming, the penguins went back to the Montreal Biodome, where they continue to help the public appreciate their species. Hopefully, seeing them in the biodome will inspire visitors to protect the gentoo penguins' natural habitat and ecosystem.

We did some incredible things for the filming of *Mr. Popper's Penguins*. I enjoyed being with the penguins and have fond memories. It was a treat to learn to recognize all their personalities and interact with each of them. And, of course, we had to hang out in the cold. It was the penguins' world, after all.

Tips for Training Animals from Larry Madrid

Learn the behaviors and tendencies of birds or whatever animal you want to train. Then get to know the animal as an individual. Trainers call this "reading" an animal. Read an animal's personality and motivation. Get inside your pet's head.

You are there for the animals and want training to help you bond with them. Be your pets' partner, and they will want to learn.

Chapter 9

CLAIRE DORÉ
(PALMDALE, CALIFORNIA)

Bonny in director's chair (where she belongs)

Bonny as the Shih Tzu in *Seven Psychopaths*
PAWSCAR Award Winner

Claire Doré

Dogs love to eat. They will do just about anything for treats, right? Not always.

Bonny the shih tzu, weighing in at seven pounds, taught me better. The little imperial shih tzu, who has white with brown fur around her ears, deep brown eyes, and an elfin face, was only ten months old when she entered my life. This adorable puppy turned out to be the most challenging dog I've trained in more than ten years as a movie animal trainer.

In the dark comedy *Seven Psychopaths*, Marty (Colin Farrell) looks for inspiration to pull him out of his writer's block and stumbles into a criminal element in Los Angeles. He gets caught up in a scheme that involves Billy (Sam Rockwell) and Hans (Christopher Walken) kidnapping gangster Charlie's (Woody Harrelson) beloved shih tzu (Bonny).

The movie's writer/director, Martin McDonagh, wanted a small, quiet little shih tzu for the role of Bonny. I am an animal trainer with Cathy Pittman's company, Performing Animal Troupe. Cathy found Bonny, who seemed to have the perfect personality for the role, and rescued her. I brought Bonny to Martin. When he met her, he immediately fell in love with Bonny and agreed with our choice. Although Cathy had adopted the dog and Bonny belongs to Performing Animal Troupe, Cathy wanted her to live with me. Bonny quickly became part of my family of pets. I gladly became her mommy and trainer.

Becoming a Trainer

My interest in training animal actors started when I was sixteen years old in Vancouver, Canada, and our high school class assignment was to interview someone about their career. I interviewed a local studio-animal trainer who trained animals for movies and television; a studio animal is specifically trained to work in those two media. After talking to the trainer and watching another at work, I became obsessed with the goal of becoming a studio-animal trainer.

I was too young to have formal college education in animal training, so during my next two years of high school, when I had spare time, I made a hobby out of training my family pets and my neighbors' pets. I volunteered at our local zoo and wildlife rehabilitation facilities. I avidly read every book I could find on the subject of animal training and obsessively studied behavioral modification and operant conditioning, which in its positive form involves associating certain behaviors with positive consequences. Nothing brought me greater joy than to learn as much as possible.

After graduating from high school, I worked for a studio-animal company, where I was responsible for feeding and cleaning up after five tigers, a lion, a jaguar, nine wolves, four bears, two raccoons, a fox, and several birds of prey. It was very messy work in freezing cold Canadian winter conditions, but I was ecstatically happy to be there. When I was nineteen years old, I was accepted into the Exotic Animal Training and Management Program at Moorpark College near Los Angeles.

> **DID YOU KNOW...?**
>
> In 1943, the iconic long-haired collie Lassie became an animal star in *Lassie, Come Home.*

Many people think that studio-animal training would be the greatest career because they envision themselves playing with animals all day. But this kind of work takes over a person's life. Animals never take time off from their needs, and movies are shot on location for long days and nights. So it can be difficult on a trainer's social life. Studio-animal training is an exceptionally tough field to break into and even harder to continue making a living at. The conventional wisdom is that if you can be happy doing anything else, focus on pursuing that goal instead. But if you have a burning drive, you just might make it happen.

Attending a professional animal-training school can make it easier for an aspiring trainer to volunteer with studio-animal companies in order to learn the craft. Apprenticeship is an important element of the job. Because this was my passion and I wasn't drawn to do anything else, I pursued my career slowly but surely over a period of many years. I wanted to experience, see, and absorb everything that was part of this job, on and off set. Getting to the point where I could actually support myself as a studio-animal trainer required that kind of dedication and, dare I say, obsession.

Training Bonny

I drew on all my hard-won previous experience to train Bonny. She'd had absolutely no training before Cathy found her, and we had only five weeks to prepare for her first movie role. After working with her for a while, I began to think of Bonny as a quirky, fluffy little lapdog with only two settings — off and, occasionally, on. She liked to lie around most of the day, like a little piece of carpet, and roll over on her side to take naps in some of the strangest places, such as in the middle of the kitchen floor or behind furniture and wedged against the wall. She interspersed sleeping with occasional short bursts of energy.

Bonny the shih tzu.

There were days when I would look at the script and think, "This will be easy. There is very little action. All Bonny has to do is hang around or be held. She's supposed to lie on a couch, a table, or a bar. No problem." However, one scene in *Seven Psychopaths* required Bonny to sleep next to Christopher Walken's character. The fact that a dog loves to do something, such as nap — Bonny's favorite pastime — doesn't mean she'll always be ready to do it on cue. As we prepared for what should have been a quietly intimate bonding moment between actor and dog, Bonny had a sudden burst of puppy energy. None of the crew had ever seen her move so fast. I was able to entice her to relax by gently bouncing her like a baby on my knee. Knowing that she tended to mimic me, I breathed deeply, and she did the same until she calmed down and was prepared for her sleeping scene.

Motivating Bonny

The image most people have of a trainer is a person who reaches into the pouch attached to her belt and selects morsels of food that the dog eagerly gobbles down. One of the biggest challenges in training Bonny, at this point in her career, was that food rarely motivated her. How I missed dogs who learned whatever I taught so they could receive their supply of goodies!

Sometimes, dogs will try to push a trainer's buttons and play psychological games with them. The way Bonny thinks is much simpler. She has a stubborn streak but is never malicious. With only two weeks before I could start preliminary training with her, she still had me trying to figure out what she liked to eat.

At times, Bonny seemed more like an independent cat than an easy-to-please canine. While attempting to discover what would motivate her, I learned that she disliked chicken, steak, bacon, sausage, canned dog food, most commercial dog treats, and pretty much anything else that dogs typically go crazy for. She occasionally enjoyed crunchy dog biscuits. Because she was still growing, she needed nutrition and supplements, and I made sure she got her daily requirements. Sometimes, though, at the beginning of a workday, I'd feel nervous because she had refused all her treats.

It was always a little game to lure Bonny into taking that first bite of a treat. If she decided to chew and swallow a certain food, it was her stamp of approval. That day, she would work for this particular food for a while, maybe throughout the training session, until it no longer pleased her. Then she would spit it out. She showed no consistency in what she preferred. One day, the magic treat might be Kraft Singles. The next day, she couldn't care less about cheese slices.

Bonny's palate and personality kept me constantly trying to find what would keep her interested. Because she was such a picky eater, I did much of her training without using food as a reward. To add to the challenge, she wasn't toy motivated, though her food and toy motivation grew slowly while we prepped for her film debut. Fortunately, by the time the shoot began, I knew Bonny well, and she had bonded to me enough that I could motivate her with excited praise and cuddles, even if she didn't feel like taking treats.

Bonny's Friends

On the set, Bonny became important to the crew, and they connected with her as a member of their family. Having a cute dog to pet and cuddle was good for morale and relieved stress. I allowed everyone, if they had the time, to connect with her.

Actors enjoyed working with Bonny because she wasn't constantly looking for direction. She was like any other good actor and naturally related to or deferred to her costars rather than upstaging them. Although she could be a bit of a diva over which food she preferred, as an animal actor, she was always generous and did not take anything away from the human actors' performances.

Woody Harrelson's character, a vicious mob boss, owned the dog. His affection for her made a comic contrast to his "profession." I knew it was important for him to bond with Bonny, so Woody spent time getting to know her. Having a real and loving relationship helped him get into the emotions of loss that his character felt when the criminals stole his dog. Bonny's other main relationships were with Sam Rockwell, Colin Farrell, and Christopher Walken, who kindly said to me at one point, "This is the greatest dog I've ever worked with."

Owen (left) and
Bonny (right) at home

There are so many elements to any production. I believe that our job, as animal trainers, should be to make it easier for everyone else, with a minimum of interference. We must connect with people and become part of the crew. The directors and producers have so much to deal with, and we're only one element of the whole project. There are, of course, some ego issues in the film industry, but trainers don't need to be part of them. It is essential to blend with and complement what everyone else is doing, while making sure the animal is set up to succeed.

Also, one of our jobs as trainers is to make sure it is safe for the animals. That's why I love having American Humane Association certified animal safety representatives on set. Since producers hire animal trainers, it can be difficult for us to tell them we can't do what they want. A lot of people in production are also concerned about safety for the animals, but getting the shot they want is their biggest priority.

For me, training animal actors is more of a lifestyle than a career. Currently, Bonny and I live with several other dogs, including Iris (a terrier mix) and Owen (a golden retriever), cats, two pet rats, a tortoise, and a twenty-gallon tank of Madagascar hissing cockroaches. At first, Bonny didn't know how to play with my other dogs. She would get hyperactive and jump around and on them. One of my smaller dogs patiently taught her how to play normally. Now Bonny has a better understanding of the dogs' behavior and gets along well with everybody.

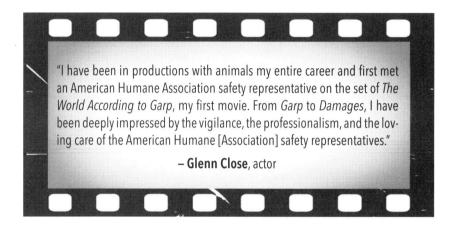

"I have been in productions with animals my entire career and first met an American Humane Association safety representative on the set of *The World According to Garp*, my first movie. From *Garp* to *Damages*, I have been deeply impressed by the vigilance, the professionalism, and the loving care of the American Humane [Association] safety representatives."

— **Glenn Close**, actor

Bonny's Moment

About seven months after filming was completed, Performing Animal Troupe was contacted about having Bonny appear at the world premiere of *Seven Psychopaths* at the Toronto International Film Festival. I traveled with Bonny to Toronto, where she met a variety of members of the press and was reunited with her costars on the red carpet. I was so proud of how she calmly faced the potentially intimidating barrage of cameras and reporters when posing for her pictures. She repeated this feat at the U.S. premiere a few months later in Beverly Hills, marking the official studio release of the film.

Since her star turn in *Seven Psychopaths*, Bonny has been in commercials for WatchESPN, Capital One, Skechers, and *Reader's Digest*. She has appeared on the TV shows *Key & Peele*, *2 Broke Girls*, and *Jimmy Kimmel Live*. Now she even has her own Facebook page with thousands of likes. Bonny also works as a certified pet-therapy dog, visiting a veterans' home in Los Angeles through a program called Reconnecting with Our Military Personnel (ROMP). She starred in a supercute calendar for Old Friends Animal Shelter and Education Center (www.oldfriends rescue.org), of which ROMP is a satellite program.

Bonny on a bus bench
with her movie poster

Cathy and I were thrilled when American Humane Association awarded Bonny its prestigious PAWSCAR Award (the organization's answer to the Oscars) for Best Animal in a Leading Role. They cited Bonny's pivotal role in *Seven Psychopaths* as the dog who spurred the story's action and attracted the attention of every character in the movie.

Bonny is a very simple little creature with a serene nature and beautiful soul. It's only after she gets to know someone that she reveals loads of personality — a trait that has impressed me as one of her most endearing qualities. She is so very precious, and it's been such a rewarding experience working with her.

Tips for Training Hard-to-Motivate Dogs from Claire Doré

Dogs who aren't easily motivated by food or toys can still be trained. Get to know what makes your dog's tail wag. Does your dog react eagerly when you talk to or praise him in an excited tone of voice? Does he have a favorite spot where he loves to be scratched or petted? Does she love it when you speak baby talk to her? Over time and with careful observation,

Claire Doré with
Iris (left) and Owen
(right)

you will learn some of your dog's favorite motivators, *besides* toys and treats, to use as rewards.

In order for these forms of motivation to work best, the trainer has to try to become the center of a dog's world. This means spending as much positive time together as possible. Your dog should view you as a person who is fun and with whom he or she always feels happy and safe. You want to be someone your dog can look to for guidance, since dogs seek the approval of humans with whom they have mutually loving and respectful relationships. The stronger your relationship with your dog, the more effective alternative rewards will be.

Carrie Carrot and Harry as
Tom Waits's Rabbit in *Seven Psychopaths*
A Constant Companion

Claire Doré

My first experience training rabbits was for a Disney television series called *So Weird*. I crawled under my desk to retrieve the show's giant fifteen-pound Flemish rabbit, who was hiding there. She whipped around and kicked me in the head. I wound up with a mild concussion. The injury didn't give me a phobia, but I was not too comfortable around rabbits anymore. So when I got the assignment to train two rabbits for the movie *Seven Psychopaths*, and also work with the fifty-two other rabbits we used for one scene, I was understandably filled with trepidation.

In the movie, Zachariah, played by musician Tom Waits, carries a white rabbit with him everywhere. Zachariah is part of the cast of

Harry (left) and
Carrie Carrot (right)

deranged but somehow likable characters who steal a dog (Bonny) from a gangster (Woody Harrelson).

Performing Animal Troupe, a studio-animal company owned by Cathy Pittman, trained and supplied all the movie's animals. Cathy's two young, blue-eyed rex rabbits, who would eventually be nicknamed Carrie Carrot and Harry, were cast as the main rabbit. They would interchangeably play the role of Zachariah's constant rabbit companion.

When we got the rabbits, the female was still raising some babies, whom we also adopted. I'd never had experience with baby rabbits and found them to be the most precious creatures on the planet. Spending even ten minutes snuggling a rabbit is a sure way of brightening anyone's day.

In one scene, a flashback, Zachariah visits a character who is keeping fifty-two white rabbits in his yard. Because adult rabbits frequently hump each other as a dominance behavior, and this would not have worked for the movie, we ended up using fifty-two juvenile rabbits of a larger species, New Zealand whites. They wouldn't be old enough to display dominance behavior and would match the hero rabbits in size.

Since I was to be their trainer, the rex rabbits came home to live with

Carrie Carrot and Bonny, the shih tzu in *Seven Psychopaths*

me. While they didn't have much interaction with my other animals, my dogs and cats found them fascinating. The rabbits had a room to themselves, but they didn't seem to mind occasional canine and cat attention. I housed them in extra-large dog crates, customized with shelves and cardboard-box dens.

Q: How Do You Train a Rabbit? A: Very Carefully

While training the rabbits, I witnessed some funny behaviors. They had to learn to run from one small crate into another, at the sound of a buzzer, for a food reward. The female rabbit would finish her snack, bring her dish to the front, and chuck it at the crate door. This was her way of letting me know she had finished her treat and was ready for the next task and reward. Another thing she did to express herself was to greet me by putting her front paws up on the door of the large crate she was housed in. When I opened it, she would nudge me like a puppy dog, as if asking to be petted.

The rabbits had to be conditioned into trusting that they would always be kept safe. A tough job. For a defenseless rabbit, everything is dangerous. We planned to use a fake rabbit for scenes that might frighten the rex rabbits. But because they became so comfortable prior to filming, Tom was able to carry and hold them safely through every scene.

For the movie, Tom would be carrying the rabbits constantly, so I had to prepare by socializing them. The script even called for Tom to run with the rabbit through a fiery shoot-out. To accustom them to a variety of environments, I took the rabbits to different places and exposed them to moving objects, such as a garage door opening and closing.

The rabbits' diet was usually hay and alfalfa pellets. Their metabolism is so high that they required hay for calories. I temporarily took away the pellets so I could use them as a motivation for learning behaviors the rabbits had to perform. To get them to run, I used the alfalfa pellets and chopped apples as special treats for positive reinforcement.

Rabbits desire sanctuary. This natural instinct can be used in training. They want to be in an enclosed area instead of out in the open where they are easy prey. Rabbits in the wild naturally fear that predators will swoop down from the sky and grab them. These rabbits had never been attacked, but they still had the instinct to seek shelter. I needed the rabbits to run on cue. They learned to hop to their kennel when they heard my buzzer cue, to feel the security of their kennel and get the little treats they liked. Between filming scenes, they liked to continue hanging out in their kennels, where they felt safe and comfortable.

I enjoyed watching Tom transform into a kind of "rabbit whisperer." I would offer to hold the rabbits between takes, but Tom almost always wanted to pet and keep them in his arms. Most of his scenes were with the female rabbit he named Carrie Carrot. I started calling the male rabbit Harry to rhyme with "Carrie."

Harry wasn't as personable as Carrie. With her exceptionally mellow personality, Carrie loved Tom's touch. She closed her eyes and relaxed as Tom cuddled her. Harry was more hormonal. His instincts told him to be warier. This made him less focused on Tom and not as sociable as Carrie.

After the Show

Carrie Carrot and Harry now each live with rabbits of their own sex (no more mating). They have their own yard and hutch. Carrie's hutch mates are her daughters, Mary and Sherry; Harry is housed with his son, Larry. They all reside at the Performing Animal Troupe ranch.

I have worked with Carrie on a few smaller jobs and always love reconnecting with her. On one special occasion, Carrie and Harry and their children, all fully grown, got to work together in a Skechers ad. I called this the "Carrot Family Reunion" shoot.

Seven Psychopaths premiered at the Toronto International Film Festival on September 7, 2012. Both Carrie and Bonny the shih tzu made it onto the movie's poster. Tom Waits's character even refers to Carrie by name in the movie.

Although my first experience with the Flemish rabbit who kicked me in the head made me wary, I am so grateful I got to work with Carrie Carrot and Harry. Getting to know and appreciate their distinctive personalities turned me into a rabbit fan for life.

Tips for Training Rabbits
from Claire Doré

Figure out your rabbits' favorite treats by offering them a variety of foods, such as rabbit treats that pet stores sell or chopped fruit. Give the treats in small amounts and watch what they choose. Apples, bananas, and strawberries are often favorites, but rabbits, like people, have different tastes. This process may take a while, as some rabbits can be finicky. Sometimes, they're initially only comfortable eating their regular food. Many of the fruits that rabbits love, as well as some of their favorite veggies, like carrots, are high in sucrose. Use tiny morsels of these favorite foods for treats so they don't get too much sugar in their diet.

After you find treats that your rabbits like, you can guide them with the treats to do certain things, such as come to you, turn in a circle, or sit up tall. Give them the treats when they correctly do what you've asked.

Because rabbits can have short attention spans, start training them with very small steps. Guide them toward you from a one-foot distance or have them turn a half circle or sit up only partway.

Keep sessions short and fun for your rabbit friends.

Chapter 10

STEVE MARTIN

(FRAZIER PARK, CALIFORNIA)

From left to right: Cody, Harley, Thunder, and Shadow

Thunder, Harley, Shadow, and Cody
as the Wolves of *True Blood, The Vampire Diaries, Teen Wolf*, and *Game of Thrones*
Walking on the Wild Side

Steve Martin

In *True Blood*, the hit HBO series, the folks of Bon Temps, Louisiana, are always besieged by something scary or weird. Not only do vampires inhabit their town, but also werewolves live in this murky fantasy universe. Alcide, played by classically trained actor Joe Manganiello, transforms into a werewolf, which is our 120-pound wolf Thunder. At Working Wildlife, my trainers and I train and work with Thunder and many of the other wolves people see in movies and on television.

We built our current Working Wildlife facility in 1990. It covers over sixty acres, with housing and exercise space for wolves, leopards, tigers, lions, chimps, zebras, and even feral cats and raccoons. The wolves live in individual housing, each with a den box where they can sleep comfortably. They have large outside run areas and a big yard with obstacles, stairways, pipes, and raised platforms. The wolves make up many games to play and chase each other for hours. One will pick up a stick, the others will chase him, and they all run until they are tired. They stand and growl as if saying, "Go ahead. Try to take this stick from me."

Training is not an adequate term for all that our staff does. Their relationships with the animals are much broader and deeper than what is usually associated with training. The professional trainers at Working Wildlife go out for walks with the wolves and introduce the wolf pups to new people. They expose them to a variety of people and situations. That way, when they are taken to a set, nothing is strange or new enough to scare the animals. Our wolves grow up with the attitude "Everybody is my buddy." Trainers get to know the wolves' personalities and enjoy

Steve Martin with Harley (left) and Shadow (right) at Working Wildlife ranch

having working and friendly relationships with them. One of our trainers has such a good rapport with the bears and wolves that he even wrestles with the bears.

Paul Newman, Clint Black, and Lisa Hartman are some of the celebrities who have come out to Working Wildlife to meet their animal costars. Joe Manganiello visited the ranch several times and got to know the wolves and observe them. He talked to Chris, one of the trainers, and used what he learned to help him prepare for his role as the werewolf Alcide on *True Blood*.

Joe and his girlfriend walked around with the wolf Thunder, who would be his werewolf alter ego. I told him, "Let the wolf come to you. Make it very low-key. Reach down and pet Thunder. On the walk, say, 'Good boy' to him. Let him make the decision about where to walk."

Most celebrities are nice, normal people. They have their good and bad days like the rest of us. On set, before the wolves are in a scene, actors walk around and pet them, with trainers nearby, to create a comfortable atmosphere for human and animal actors.

Care for Life

I have a twenty-year-old female tiger named Sasha. She has been blind for two years. She's a nice animal but is old and has a little bit of arthritis. So she gets to relax and enjoy her later years with us. The trainers and handlers take our retired animals to schools and other places for educational purposes, so the animals lead rewarding lives even in retirement. As long as animal actors are healthy and active, we let them work all their lives.

Ivory, one of our black leopards, is twenty-one years old. He's a "mama's boy" who bonded deeply with my wife, Donna Martin. We came to think of Ivory's littermate Crystal as a "daddy's girl." Donna and I hand-raised Ivory and Crystal from the time they were six weeks old, walking them on leashes. We conditioned them to working around cameras, wires, and boom mics by taking the leopards nearly everywhere and often visiting movie sets. The level of love, commitment, and trust Donna and I built helped to turn them into the leopards of choice for many productions.

For a scene in *True Blood*, Ivory did a full snarl — showing his ivories — only a foot away from a main character's face. Our two seasoned movie animals always enjoyed performing. It stimulated their minds. When they saw the cameras and lighting on set, they came alive, just as human actors do.

Crystal had been healthy except for a birth anomaly. Instead of a classic fluffy and thick leopard's tail, hers had a thin, pointy tip that enticed her to occasionally suck at it. Unlike zoo animals, who sometimes lick their tails out of boredom, Crystal never chewed on or caused hers to bleed. One night, we had an unusually big snowstorm for Southern California. Ivory and Crystal snuggled in their cozy, heated den boxes; but somehow, Crystal's tail got wet, and she began to suck on it. The bone at the tip broke through about a half inch. Our veterinarian had to amputate the tip of her tail.

While Crystal recovered, Donna watched her around the clock so the leopard wouldn't lick the surgery site when it started itching. Crystal loved having Donna's full attention!

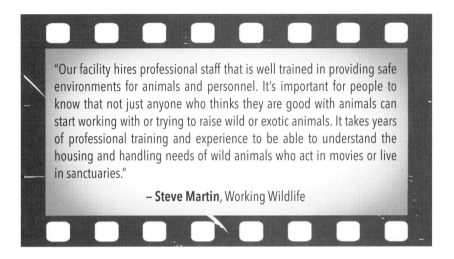

"Our facility hires professional staff that is well trained in providing safe environments for animals and personnel. It's important for people to know that not just anyone who thinks they are good with animals can start working with or trying to raise wild or exotic animals. It takes years of professional training and experience to be able to understand the housing and handling needs of wild animals who act in movies or live in sanctuaries."

— **Steve Martin**, Working Wildlife

Handling Wolves and Other Wild Animals

My career training animals began when I was in high school. After graduating, I went to work with a company owned by Ralph Helfer. He and Ivan Tors, the producer of *Flipper* and *Sea Hunt*, teamed up and expanded each of their companies to produce the television series *Daktari*, which featured a veterinarian running an animal study center in Africa. I worked on that project as well as other commercials and films for four or five years and started acquiring various animals. Dog-training work helped me stay afloat until I could start Working Wildlife in 1973 in Acton, California. I launched the facility with a large nursery of baby tigers, bears, lions, orangutans, and chimps, until I had over one hundred animals.

Raising animals from babies causes them not to be so dangerous later in life. It also gives me a better understanding of how to work with them, including what I can and can't do. At first, I felt intimidated by the large cats and bears, but I got to watch them grow and observe their personalities forming.

It is illegal to capture, and remove from the wild, wolves and other wild animals. Often, the California Department of Fish and Wildlife comes to the facility we have now in Frazier Park with abandoned young wolves, when it is not possible to rehabilitate or return them to their natural habitats. We also care for young deer and baby bears that the agency brings to us. Most of our animals have been born in captivity, never having had to survive on their own, and we get them from reputable breeders of their species.

The Convention on International Trade in Endangered Species of Wild Fauna and Flora (CITES) issues passports for wild and exotic animals that confirm where the animals came from and that they have not been stolen or captured. They also use microchips to identify the animals and document their origins. We must renew the animals' CITES passports regularly at a cost of $150 per animal. We have not worked or traveled out of the country with our animals for years, but we still keep up their CITES passports.

Wolves at Work

When we arrive at Working Wildlife ranch to bring the wolves to a set, the animals get excited. They pace back and forth, waiting their turn to get into the van. Acting work is exciting and fun for the wolves. Unlike animals living in zoos, ours get out and go places. They're gone for months at a time on location. The work they do interests them. On set, we keep the wolves active and exercise them every day.

Harley

Wolves are very smart. Often, they do things better than we expected or trained for. Before going to a set, they learn animal actor basics: finding their mark and standing on it; stopping, looking, growling, turning, and exiting; running behind a camera car; and running on course through parks and woods and around houses. My trainers and I only condition animals to new environments and train with positive reinforcement such as food rewards and praise — "Good pet," "Good boy." We never force an animal. We treat our wolves with care, love, and affection. They especially like dog biscuits.

Shadow

It is important to wolves to be part of the group, have affection, know their pecking order, and socialize. We clean, talk to, and scratch them. We get to know them as individuals. Relationships are an important part of this work. The animals look forward to our visits. Every time they see us, they expect a greeting. After all, we are coming to their home. The least we can do is say hi to each of them. They say hi right back.

Anything we teach the wolves becomes their "acting thing." They start volunteering certain behaviors. It's obvious that they are thinking about how to get rewards, because they spontaneously present behaviors to the trainers. Shadow, a black wolf, and Harley, a gray wolf, are exceptionally good at drawing attention to what they can do. On set, they'll find something like a rock or piece of wood and stand on it for as long as twenty minutes, waiting to be "paid" for staying on their mark. If no one pays attention to Shadow on his mark, he'll leave it, come over to a trainer, and run back to the mark, as if he's saying, "Now look at me. Where is my food?"

If the crew works in a wooded area, Shadow and Harley grab a stick in their mouths, step back five feet, and invite the trainers for a play-and-chase game. They also like chasing each other's tails. Yet they know the difference between play and work, and get serious and focused when it is time to do a scene.

Harley likes almost everybody. We can put him on a harness or a leash, and he readily goes on walks with actors to get them used to being with a wolf. Shadow is laid-back. Cody, Harley, and Thunder are all very smart. Thunder is light brown. He's a little standoffish with people he doesn't know. He is also the steadiest and best at staying on his mark. Cody, Harley, and Thunder are from the same litter. We work with Shadow and Harley together because they are both outgoing with great attitudes.

"Dangerous" Scenes with Wolves

Movie wolves have to be able to repeat actions that constitute a fake yet believable wolf attack. Even though Shadow, who came to us from the East Coast as a baby, may seem aggressive and snarling on TV shows and movies, he has a nice personality. All his aggressive behaviors are created. Shadow knows snarling is a big game. When we do a setup with a green screen for computer-generated imagery (CGI), such as the kind used with him on *Game of Thrones*, I put a bone down near Shadow. Then I act as if I'm going to take the bone away from him. He snarls, even though we have played like this hundreds of times and I have never actually taken his bone. After the snarl, I say, "Good boy," and give him the bone.

Repeatedly doing this series of actions teaches the wolves the game. Afterward, they have no animosity toward me and do not hold grudges. Instead, since their instinct is to lick the chin of the dominant wolf, they lick my face with affection. Chris, one of our trainers, has a beard, and the wolves love to lick it. In the wild, wolves roll over on their backs for the dominant wolf. At the ranch, they live in packs, and we leave their pecking order up to them; but if two wolves are rivals, we don't put them together. We eliminate dominance problems before they become bigger issues.

Although the wolves on *True Blood*, *The Vampire Diaries*, *Teen Wolf*, *Game of Thrones*, and other programs are portrayed as menacing and dangerous, they develop a very social bond with their trainers. We teach the wolves to stop, look, growl, turn, and exit. When we say, "All right," they turn and leave.

For scenes where the wolves appear to be chasing someone or something, they are running, unleashed, behind us. We ride in camera cars, calling to the wolves. The director calls cut, we put the wolves' leashes back on, and they get paid with food. Then we return to the starting point, unleash the wolves, and do the chase scene all over again.

Keeping Wolves and Humans Safe and Content

After we read the script for a new project, we practice with the wolves until the animals are very comfortable doing whatever is required. We think about the locations and all the variables. What will keep them safe? How can we most effectively portray actions without anyone getting hurt?

For filming *The Bourne Legacy*, we brought Cody, Thunder, Harley, Shadow, Sage, and Frankie, and two wolf-dog hybrids, Maverick and Rugby. The wolves had to perform a scene in the cold, snowy mountain location outside Calgary, which was supposed to represent Alaska. The film crew wanted Harley to walk with a certain cadence while snarling and looking in a certain direction and going to his mark. These actions would make it look as if Harley was making eye contact with the actor. The people filming the scene had firm ideas about what they wanted to achieve, so they shot it repeatedly. Harley did the same walk, snarling and hitting his mark each time. For sixteen takes, he performed at the level of perfection, and he was still willing to repeat the scene. But I said, "The wolf has performed enough for the day and needs to take a break."

My trainers and I always make sure camera crews and the wolves are kept away from each other. We check constantly to make sure no one is around the wolves, even in parks when the animals are running loose for a scene.

If the script calls for a wolf to snarl only inches from an actor's face, we use a hybrid wolf-dog so there is less chance of something going wrong. A wolf might accidentally snap at a person instead of the food that we're using as a reward for the snarl.

We carefully examine the set where the wolves will perform. We ask that the set have no food, plastic spoons, forks, bags, or anything rubber because wolves will eat whatever is lying around on the ground or buried. They will quickly crunch up and swallow plastic food containers. Eating these things can be life threatening for wolves. One time, a crew member left a plastic spoon on a site, and Harley found it and started chewing. It could have killed him. I had repeatedly told the crew, "Don't leave any items with food smells where the wolves will be." We check the ground, foot by foot. A pack of wolves will smell and dig up any area where they smell food or urination. Also, on a property where a set has been built, there might be rat poison that people have put out. We have to be alert to every possible danger. American Humane Association certified animal safety representatives are on the set when our wolves or other animals are working. They make sure everything is being done properly.

Animal Ambassadors

At Working Wildlife, we introduce wild animals to kids who come out here from local schools. Sometimes, three to five school buses, filled with children, arrive. We take the kids and teachers around, and they get to see the animals close-up. The kids have a personal, often profound, experience with them. The children are changed for the better; they leave with a deeper understanding and appreciation of wildlife.

Animals are the stars in film and television. I believe they are ambassadors of awareness for the public, especially to people who live in cities and may never see animals in the wild. Animals do not abuse the earth. They remind us all that we are sharing the planet with them.

If humans destroyed the animals' environments, it would be a sad world with only people left. Each species was put here for a reason. We must respect what animals are and let them be who they are. We are only a small part of this world.

Tips for Training Animals from Steve Martin

All animals have their own intelligence level. Bears are extremely smart. Cats are intelligent but at a more primitive level. Wolves work together and are very aware of everything around them. They are extremely sensitive to their environments.

I think one of the biggest things in training is to always be patient. When the animal likes doing the task or trick, he will start offering it to you.

Use a positive approach. If you ask a dog to put his paw up, think about how to ask with consistency so the animal will not be confused. When you are consistent, training will go a lot faster, and the animals will enjoy it.

Part 3

DOG STARS
AND THEIR TRAINERS

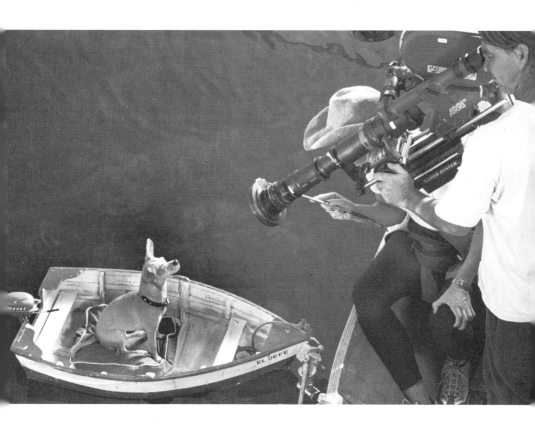

Gidget on the set of *Legally Blonde 2: Red, White & Blonde*

By 1924, Rin Tin Tin had become a major canine film hero for both the moviegoing public and the financially failing Warner Bros. studio. In Susan Orlean's book *Rin Tin Tin: The Life and the Legend*, she writes about the death of the original Rinty in 1932. The next day, radio networks nationwide broadcast an hour-long program about the dog. She says, "Theaters posted death notices in their windows, as if they had lost a member of the family. Every newspaper ran an obituary and, in many cases, a long feature detailing the dog's career, as if his life had defined a time period that was now at an end."

In her book, Orlean's historical account of dogs in movies is fascinating, from sequenced photographs in 1882 to the first dog featured in a film in 1895. The first animal hero on film came in the form of a collie who was featured in the British film *Rescued by Rover*.

Dogs, as icons of love, loyalty, and devotion, make ideal animal stars. But when they are working on film sets, the qualities that make dogs unique and invaluable to humans also require people who understand how canines experience the world around them.

> **DID YOU KNOW...?**
>
> In 1972, a Charles Schulz *Peanuts* cartoon showed its approval of American Humane Association by featuring Snoopy making out his will and leaving all his belongings to the organization.

Picture this: a film set with actors, directors, producers, makeup artists, hairstylists, costumers, food preparation, camera operators, equipment, technicians, and any number of sights, sounds, and smells. Did we say smells? That's where movie dogs perk up. While the humans on set have only 5 million scent receptors, the canine actors have 125 to 300 million. Every whiff of perfume, costume fabric, hair spray, chemical, and food communicates to a dog's nose, "Smell me. Catalog me in your doggy brain. Don't bother thinking about what your trainer wants you to do. Pay attention to me instead."

Robin Ganzert with the current Rin Tin Tin, closing the New York Stock Exchange on September 7, 2011

Dogs on set are interacting with a movie world through their senses. Even more pertinent to their performance than those yummy food smells from craft services are the myriad of possible objects or actions that could hurt them.

Trainers must consider where they will position themselves while the dog is in a scene. From an off-camera location, they watch the action, ensure the dog is safe, and give cues and rewards. The best trainers consider how to make it look as if a movie dog is relating to the actor and not the trainer. They wonder, "What emotions and actions of the actor will affect my dog? Will I be limited to only hand signals, or can I speak to the dog? Are there things happening in the scene that will affect the dog's performance or concentration? Will something scare the dog? How fast and carefully can I teach the dog new behaviors if the director wants changes right away?"

Observing the Dogs on Set

I (Robin) visited a movie set that had been built in a neighborhood in the midst of real houses and apartments. Curious adults and children gathered around to watch the scene. Props were noisily delivered. Preparing for the shoot created excitement.

The busy atmosphere of a movie set doesn't have to generate anxiety for professionally trained animals. Professional animal actors learn how to cope with and are desensitized to cameras swinging down, sets being built or repaired, microphones looking like fluffy toys, people milling around, and any number of strange things happening. They are taught to pay attention to and, even more important, to trust the trainer.

The scene I observed re-created a pit-bull attack. American Humane Association (AHA) safety representatives met with producers in preproduction to make detailed plans, but due to the risky nature of the scene, the production team was sensitive and on edge that day. Now the trainer was conferring with the AHA safety representative on set about how to film the scene without any dogs or human actors being harmed. The calming presence of Ken Gold, PhD, a twenty-year veteran of the AHA Film and Television Unit, allowed the scene to be rehearsed and shot on the same day without any problems for the dogs or human stars.

Dogs Need Protection

AHA safety representative Beth Langhorst says that she's grateful for the relatively new laser thermometers that measure the temperature of a surface. "One time, on a beach, the director said a dog should sit on the sand while the crew set up a scene," Beth recalls. "I reminded him that the ground was very hot. The director insisted. He wanted the dog to stay on the sand until the actress arrived for the scene. In this type of situation, I used to ask the director to take off his shoes and socks and stand on the sand for ten minutes. If he wasn't dancing, we would let the dog stand there. They get my point, and we don't bring in the dogs until the directors are ready for them to perform. I like having the laser thermometers. It's easier to demonstrate to the director that it's far too hot for the animal actor."

In the following section of this book, you will read about Uggie from *The Artist*; Benji of the world-renowned Benji projects; Gidget, the Taco Bell dog; and other celebrity canines who have literally carried films on their small shoulders. These dogs are loaded with personality. You'll be glad to know that no matter what situation canine cuties are involved with, on big or small screens, people with the necessary love, know-how, and authority are working behind the scenes to protect them.

Chapter 11

OMAR VON MULLER
(PANORAMA CITY, CALIFORNIA)

and SARAH CLIFFORD
(CANYON COUNTY, CALIFORNIA)

Uggie (left) and Jumpy (right)

Uggie as the Jack Russell Terrier
in *The Artist,* and Jumpy
A Family of Dog Stars

Omar von Muller

One day in 2002, a friend called me and said, "There is this really nice Jack Russell who has a family, but they are getting ready to take him to the pound because he is crazy. He does bad things, like chasing their cats, and is way too hyperactive."

I said, "Just hold him for me, and I will come get him."

That family never knew what they were missing. By 2011, Uggie had won the Palm Dog Award at the Cannes Film Festival and special mention at the Prix Lumière in France for his performance as Jack, best pal of George Valentin (Jean Dujardin) in *The Artist*. Members of the British Academy of Film and Television Arts asked if they could vote for Uggie. S. T. VanAirsdale, then the editor of *Movieline*, started the "Consider Uggie" campaign on Facebook. Fans used the page to petition the Academy of Motion Picture Arts and Sciences to honor Uggie. In 2012, while *The Artist* won five Oscars, including Best Picture, Uggie napped at our home without a hint of actor ego.

Never had a member of our family received so much recognition. My wife and I would look at Uggie and ask each other, "Do you think he knows he's famous?" Uggie continued to be humble and take it all in stride. His main interests were chasing squirrels, eating sausages, and licking out empty pizza boxes.

The accolades for Uggie's performance in *The Artist* continued to roll in. *Dog News Daily* awarded our family's dog the first Golden Collar Award for Best Dog in a Theatrical Film. American Humane Association named him winner of its PAWSCAR Best Scene Stealer. On June 25, 2012, Uggie became the first dog to make his paw print on Hollywood's Walk of Fame at Grauman's Chinese Theatre. He loved the cameras

Uggie

at the event and people looking at him with appreciation. It was a very exciting day. All of this acclaim for a high-energy puppy who was on his way to a dog pound when I rescued him!

From his birth in 2000 to when we met, Uggie lived up to his reputation as an active Jack Russell terrier. That is just how his breed tends to do things. It is their nature to be energetic. People think that Jack Russells are cute — and they are — but they will tear up your apartment, chase your cat, and need a lot of exercise to keep them calm. I've seen a lot of Jack Russells being put down because people will not adopt them. Who knows where Uggie could have ended up?

Uggie the Actor

By the time Uggie came into my life, I had been training dogs for over thirty years. I had two Jack Russells, Andy and Peter, who were in many movies and commercials. Andy was an especially amazing dog. I started training Uggie and was impressed by his attention and willingness to do the work. He was an easy dog to train with positive rewards because he will eat anything. Before long, he took over all the work that Andy was getting too old to do. Uggie started his career with commercials and minor movie roles. His first big part was as Queenie in *Water for Elephants* with Robert Pattinson, Reese Witherspoon, and Christoph Waltz.

As if born to be a movie star, Uggie was always aware of being the center of attention when he heard "Action!" He didn't look at the camera but stayed focused on the scene. He put his heart into his roles. He was fearless, never hesitating to do whatever I asked of him. For *The Artist*, adaptable Uggie easily worked with Sarah Clifford, also a head trainer on the film. Set noises or other distractions did not stop him from staying in character and focused on acting.

Uggie showed remarkable interest in actors with whom he shared scenes. His talent for giving undistracted attention came about in two ways. Sometimes, his animal trainer was positioned in the right place with a shot so that Uggie appeared to be looking at the actor but was actually watching the trainer. At other times, the actor and Uggie had a strong and real bond. For example, the relationship he had with Reese Witherspoon and their mutual affection made Uggie's adoration of her natural. His devotion to Jean Dujardin was grounded in the genuine friendship that formed between them.

Uggie's offscreen signature was his love of licking people's faces. When we did presentations and made public appearances, everyone — producers, famous movie stars, moviegoers — wanted to carry Uggie and have their pictures taken with him.

After *The Artist*

Together, Uggie and I walked with the cast of *The Artist* on the red carpet at the movie's American Film Institute premiere. Uggie and I promoted the movie in London, where we were guests on *The Graham Norton Show*, and in many cities throughout the United States. We went to the Academy Awards and continued to promote the movie, traveling and meeting people who wanted to see Uggie, the dog some reviewers accused of stealing every scene he was in. We were featured in charity events and magazine photo shoots while spreading the word about the movie's stellar canine performer.

Jean Dujardin and
Uggie in *The Artist*

In 2012, Uggie's memoir, *Uggie — My Story*, was published. We launched with a book tour to London, Paris, New York, Chicago, and other cities. By then, Uggie had done cameos in a few more movies and participated in occasional promotional campaigns, but he could no longer work long days shooting films. Due to a neurological disorder, which his veterinarians could not find a cause or cure for, I had to announce Uggie's early retirement.

These days, he sleeps late and relaxes at home near our feet or gets on the couch and watches television with our daughter. We take him to the park and let him play with our seven other dogs. Outside, he is full of energy, running in the backyard until he lets himself back in through the sliding door. Just for the fun of it, he does a couple of tricks on his own when we are eating, as if he is saying, "Look at me. Now give me a treat."

If our daughter has pancakes for breakfast, we might ask him to do a trick for a bite of her food. He loves pancakes.

Uggie is going to miss a lot of cool stuff now that he is older and his movie career is over. After *The Artist* and the publication of his memoir, we received offers from all over the world for him to be in other movies. But he is having a good life. He still has his "Uggie The-Artist" Facebook page and an app. Although he continues to be a star known throughout the world, Uggie is family to us, and as he ages, it brings tears to our eyes to think about how hard it will be to lose his charming presence in our home.

And Then Came Jumpy

Today, I have a four-year-old border collie–blue heeler mix who is a YouTube sensation. The dog loves to jump great heights, and that is why we named him Jumpy. He is amazing and has the potential to be as good a movie animal actor as Uggie, or better.

I train Jumpy to do quick exercises. I never push him, or any of my animals, to learn something in one day. Rushing would be too hard on them. Jumpy started working in the industry when he was about two and a half years old, and he already has about thirty professional acting credits — music videos, commercials, and other promotions. Jumpy has a star quality similar to Uggie's. He has a natural ability and intelligence that have people asking, "How can a dog do this?"

> **DID YOU KNOW...?**
>
> In 2011, at the Beverly Hilton Hotel, American Humane Association launched the Hero Dog Awards, which would become an annual event. The program was televised on the Hallmark Channel. This celebration of the human-animal bond reaffirms the mission of the No Animals Were Harmed program.

While we have our short training sessions, I talk to Jumpy and give him rewards. He knows me so well that he learns anything quickly. His coordination is great. He's amazing at skateboarding. He does backflips and dives into a swimming pool. Every time we do something new, he surprises me with his fearless ability and desire to learn. (You can see Jumpy's videos at www.youtube.com/user/otheman62 and at

http://abcnews.go.com/blogs/lifestyle/2013/07/is-jumpy-the-most
-well-trained-dog-in-america/.)

We did a commercial in which Jumpy was supposed to freeze while chasing a ball. He had to abruptly stop running with no help from special effects. When the light shone on him, he was supposed to start running again. I could not be on the set within camera range to help him. This was the hardest shot I ever had to do with a dog. I said to Jumpy, "Wait there," and pointed to the spot where he was to come to a sudden halt. "The ball will be there, and then you should wait." There was no training other than explaining to Jumpy what the shot needed to be and where he was supposed to wait. Every take, over and over, Jumpy froze at exactly the right spot; not even a hair moved on his body. The people on the set all loved him. The clients told me that they wanted to write another commercial and do something specifically with Jumpy.

A producer called me about bringing Jumpy for a major movie role that was being filmed in Texas, but my wife was about to have our baby Sabrina, so I had to decline. Jumpy, Uggie, and I all needed to be home to welcome the newest human member of our family.

Tips for Training Dogs from Omar von Muller

Consistency and patience are the keys to successful dog training. I spend a lot of time with dogs we have rescued to help them socialize and overcome their bad experiences. I only use positive, reward-based training techniques.

Teach your dog basic obedience so he has a firm foundation and then go on to learning new commands that keep his interest.

Work in short sessions and don't expect your dog to learn something new in a day. Take your time and keep it fun by making sure your dog is enjoying what he is doing.

Remember, if a dog is instinctively high energy, this can be an asset in training, because he wants to learn new things and have work to do.

Training Uggie for *The Artist*
A Team Approach

Sarah Clifford

I knew *The Artist* would be special from the moment I read the first draft of the script but could never have guessed it would win Best Picture in the Academy Awards. The whole media experience around the film was surreal and fun. All because of one little Jack Russell named Uggie, who I am proud to have as my "nephew."

As most people concluded from meeting the world-famous Uggie on-screen or through photos and video clips of him, he is a fun, energetic, sweet dog with a great personality. Uggie is the ultimate foodie who can eat endless amounts of yummy treats — hot dogs, boiled chicken, and cooked steak — and never become full or gain weight. His love of food and his confidence were Uggie's two best traits, and the reason he was exceptionally well suited to being an animal actor. Like most terriers, he can be very stubborn, mischievous, and tenacious as well.

I met Uggie's owner and trainer, Omar von Muller, and his wife, Mercy Muller, in 2004. Through the years, we've all became close friends. Omar and I started working together when I noticed his, and his dogs', talents and skills. I offered to submit his dogs for studio projects, and a few years later added them to my website to help promote their availability. I would often submit Uggie for projects through my company, Animal Savvy. He was hired for a few jobs. The first movie I booked for him was *Wassup Rockers*, directed by Larry Clark in 2005. Uggie had a small part in which he had to chase some kids and look as if he bit one of them on the butt!

The Artist

Almost a year before *The Artist* began filming, the working title for the movie was *Beauty Spot*. Jonathan McCoy, a unit production manager

(UPM), told me about this French silent film that needed a well-trained Jack Russell terrier. At the time, the producers weren't sure it would be shot in the United States. Jonathan sent me a very early draft. Unlike other scripts that are filled with dialogue, this one made my mind become consumed with visualizing intriguing black-and-white images. Long paragraphs described scenes that would be acted without words. The project excited me, and I hoped to be a part of it.

The casting of Uggie did not happen automatically or quickly. I reached out to the film's director, Michel Hazanavicius, with a sincere email about what a wonderful and talented dog Uggie is. I said that I knew he would be perfect for the movie. Uggie performed an array of tricks that would be necessary for the role, and he had a great deal of experience working on films. I sent video links showing Uggie doing tricks such as playing dead and skateboarding.

A few months later, the producers asked to meet Uggie while they were in California scouting possible film locations. I was elated and made arrangements for them to come to Omar's house. I knew Uggie would make a good impression on them, which he did. For another several

Sarah Clifford
and Uggie

weeks, I still didn't hear anything back. Omar and I assumed that a different dog could have been cast for the role instead. Our hopes rose when a rumor started circulating among animal trainers that the producers had been looking at other Jack Russell terriers but none had impressed them as much as Uggie.

Nearly a year passed after I read the script, before I finally got the call from a new UPM, Richard Middleton. (Jonathan had decided to work on a different project.) Richard typically worked with another animal company, so I sensed his hesitation about hiring my company and me. But I wanted this project and negotiated a rate that I believed was worthy of Uggie's talents and experience.

Still, the producers and director did not commit to using Uggie just yet. Omar and I were both starting to focus our attention on other projects. Omar regularly does a Purina-sponsored tour of cities with a live show that features several of his dogs, including Uggie. He booked a gig in South America and told me that he and Uggie would be leaving the day *The Artist* was scheduled to begin filming. I was disappointed because I still wanted to work on *The Artist* more than any movie that had 'ever come my way.

On the same day I found out Uggie would be touring with Omar, Richard sent me an email finally saying they wanted Uggie for the movie. Even though Omar and Uggie hadn't left yet for South America, I felt completely crushed at the possibility that after so many emails, conversations, and meetings, I might lose this project, when we'd come so close.

I asked Omar to consider allowing me to take Uggie on the job. I offered to learn all of his training methods so I wouldn't confuse Uggie. Omar doesn't lend his dogs to other trainers for their projects, because the dogs are also part of his family — playing with the children and living in his home. He is understandably protective. It was a tough decision for Omar to make, but eventually, due to our long friendship and history of working together, he agreed to let me take Uggie and his other dog, Dash, who would be Uggie's understudy, for the duration of the film. They would stay at my house, under my care, while Omar traveled.

Preparing Uggie for *The Artist*

I began prepping with Omar as soon as I officially booked Uggie for the job. We only had three weeks before production began. We spent time each day training with the dogs and eventually with Jean Dujardin, who played the lead role of George Valentin. I knew that Jean would have to be comfortable handling Uggie to make it look believable that they had a genuine relationship.

I insisted that we have at least three full days devoted to training with Jean. I made arrangements for us to take all the dogs to Jean's rented house in the Hollywood Hills. At the same time that we were coaching Jean on how to get cozy with the dogs, we were also training Uggie to listen to me. He was used to Omar, his owner and trainer for his entire life, so it took him a few days to fully respond to me.

Uggie also bonded with Jean after a few days. Jean started to look like a natural when handling the dogs. I noticed that he picked up on the verbiage from Omar and me and imitated our tones, body language, and how we handled the dogs. This smart approach helped the dogs to view Jean as another trainer, and they responded well to him. Most actors try to befriend the dogs. Jean earned their respect in a leadership role, which made a difference in how they related to him. In a gentle way, he gained Uggie's respect.

Uggie was our lead dog. Omar's other dog, Dash, was a very young Jack Russell terrier he had adopted to double for Uggie on the film *Water for Elephants*. I decided that a third dog might be necessary. Since there were so many action scenes where Uggie had to run, we might need a stunt double to relieve Uggie and Dash and serve as a stand-in for lighting.

I searched online throughout all the California shelters for Jack Russells with markings similar to Uggie's. At the Big Bear Animal Shelter, I found a dog who looked similar to Uggie. Since he'd been there for months, the dog's time had long expired. He had been "red listed," which meant he could be euthanized at any time. I asked a friend in Big Bear to adopt Dude in case I couldn't get to the shelter soon enough. He was not a perfect match for Uggie, but I quickly began training Dude in all the basic studio behaviors and taught him the "play dead" trick.

Michel Hazanavicius shot the film in master shots with very wide frames. There wasn't a chance to replace one dog with another in quick shorts that could be edited together later. Michel sometimes did seventy or more takes for each scene. Because of the way *The Artist* was filmed, Uggie performed in the majority of the dog scenes. That little dog was always a trouper and willing to keep working, as long as there were treats involved.

On the first day, we used Dash for the opening movie-within-a-movie scene, where George has escaped from his prison cell and is running down the corridor. I used Dude for two scenes. One scene of the exterior of George's house shows Dude bursting out of a burning house to fetch the police officer for help. In another scene, it is Uggie who runs up to the officer and leads him to the smoke-filled house. Uggie also did the interior fire scenes. The second scene that features Dude is when Doris, George's upset wife, is supposed to fling a newspaper at the dog. Uggie objected to having Doris throw a paper toward him, so we substituted Dude, who was agreeable to the action, when Doris tossed a paper his way but didn't actually hit him with it.

During filming, Jean always carried treats, which he called "sausages," and rewarded Uggie for each take. He learned English words and verbal instructions the trainers used and to which Uggie responded. Equally important, Jean truly cared for Uggie.

On this film, we were always able to talk to Uggie during his scenes, since they were not recording sound. It was refreshing. On most films, we can only use hand signals while the actors speak their dialogue.

My Favorite Uggie Scenes

One day, we were filming many scenes of Jean and Uggie walking together after George's downward spiral in the story. Jean was emoting sadness, and Uggie seemed to feel that energy from him. Part of the sequence was a moment when Jean sees his battered reflection in the window of a tuxedo shop. Uggie stays at George's feet next to him.

After looking in the store window with Jean, Uggie had to walk off-leash down the sidewalk next to George. The art department must have set up five big Ritter fans on set. They blew a whirlwind of leaves and debris. The fans made it loud and extremely windy, with leaves flying everywhere. Although it must have been unsettling for Uggie, he imitated every movement Jean made, take after take. He stopped when Jean stopped, and gazed up at him. There was a moment when all of us felt the magic happen on set. A few people got teary eyed. It was cool to watch Uggie and Jean perform together in perfect harmony.

Probably the longest, most challenging, and frustrating days of the shoot were filming the vaudeville theater scene. George comes out onstage and does a trick sequence with Uggie, followed by a dance number. It took three days to film the scene. Uggie had to perform the long sequence in front of a live orchestra, in a huge theater, without being able to see me give him direction. I had to hide thirty feet away and could only verbally call out instructions to him.

By then, everyone felt cranky because we had all been working long hours. The director and first assistant director from France didn't allow any time for me to practice the sequence with Jean and Uggie before filming. They were starting to cut my rehearsal time short. I think they didn't understand the importance of what a trainer does to get a dog to perform.

I quietly agreed to go ahead, without rehearsal, and see what would happen when Uggie was free to do whatever he wanted. I told my assistant trainer, Heather, to release Uggie on our specific cue — when George comes onstage and does his opening number with Constance, his film costar. Uggie acted exactly as I'd thought he would. He breezed past Jean and trotted across the entire stage, sniffing and looking for food. Then he came to where I hid on the other side of the stage. Jean played up the humor of his canine costar ignoring him, and the flubbed scene became a well-known outtake.

After Uggie showed everyone how much he needed me, the directors allowed for my five-minute rehearsal time. I had to show Uggie the pattern, or sequence of continuous behaviors, he'd be expected to perform before arriving at his mark. After he hit the mark, he was supposed to play dead and lie on the stage, while Jean continued the act. We filmed this scene over one hundred times from multiple angles. Uggie was a trouper. Most of his takes were good, but a few of them, which were not, made it onto a funny blooper reel.

Another special day of filming was when we shot Uggie finding the cop to help George after he started to go mad and set all of his films on fire in the house. Uggie runs up to the officer, played by Joel Murray, who was very easy to work with. I coached Uggie throughout that entire scene. He had to run frantically to the cop, bark, run away, run back, grab the officer's pant leg, play dead, and run away again. Uggie impressed me that day with his ability to remember so many behaviors in the right order.

My favorite moment of filming happened during the last week, while we were shooting onstage in the interior of George's house. It's the pivotal scene, when George pulls out the gun and is about to shoot himself. Omar had returned from South America by then and was coaching Uggie to "speak" at George and "take it" to pick up George's pants leg. During one take, Uggie leaped up and grabbed Jean's entire hand in his mouth, trying to pull the gun down. Even though I am sure having a dog's teeth on his skin must have hurt him, Jean kept acting. It looked as if Uggie was truly trying to stop George from shooting himself.

I watched the scene on the video monitor with the director and crew. All of us were astonished. My mouth literally fell open, and tears filled my eyes. I had to walk away from the set to catch my breath and hide my emotion. After the director called cut, the crew was in such awe of the performance that they applauded Uggie. Poor Jean's hand was bright pink, but luckily, Uggie's teeth hadn't broken the skin. Even Omar was amazed. We still can't believe they didn't use that take. It will forever be burned in my mind as one of the most cinematic moments in film history that I've ever witnessed a dog perform.

Omar, Uggie, and I Have Our Moment

Omar was present for the first day of filming, and then he left for South America. He was gone for four weeks and came back for the final week of filming. He must have been very tired, as he got no downtime between

Gerard Butler, Uggie,
and Sarah Clifford on
the red carpet

gigs. I was running on fumes when Omar returned and was grateful to
see him. For twenty consecutive days, I'd spent fourteen to fifteen hours
on the set and then made a two-hour commute, because I live quite a distance away in a rural area. I'd go home and do two hours of farm chores,
sleep for four hours, and then start all over again.

During the final week of filming, Omar took over as Uggie's head
trainer. I continued on in a second-trainer position, helping release Uggie
into a scene when needed. Omar and I both got credited as head animal
trainers for *The Artist*, since we worked in that position, but at separate
times.

Omar and I continue to be great friends. We still work together all
the time and have a wonderful professional relationship. We recently
completed a new children's TV show pilot with five of our dogs. Omar
has taught me many valuable training skills. His lovely family and I are
very close. I see Uggie frequently, and he always expects a treat from me.
Uggie still gives stinky kisses to his "Aunt Sarah," which I enjoy.

My favorite recognition experience was accepting Uggie's Golden
Collar Award, with Omar and his daughter on the stage. To make the

night doubly thrilling, my dog Brigitte won a Golden Collar Award for Best Dog in a Television Series for her role as Stella on *Modern Family*.

I also got to go with Uggie to *Jimmy Kimmel Live* three times and really enjoyed the Weinstein Oscar party. It was a total blast and not something an animal trainer gets to experience often.

Tips for Training Dogs
from Sarah Clifford

My "secret sauce" for training dogs is to create a strong bond that is enhanced by trust, patience, and positive rewards (treats, a toy, or praise) for correct behavior. I show strong leadership and establish a level of respect.

Trust is a key element. The dog must always be able to trust that my decisions for him are reliable. During the fire sequence in *The Artist*, I asked Uggie to run into a house filled with smoke, where none of us could see anything. He had to trust that I'd never let him be unsafe.

Also, when training dogs, I use lots of repetition. And always make sure the dog has a good time!

Chapter 12

MATHILDE DE CAGNY
(LOS ANGELES, CALIFORNIA)
and EWAN MCGREGOR

Cosmo and Mathilde de Cagny

Cosmo as Arthur in *Beginners*
The Dog Who Connected a Father and Son

Mathilde de Cagny

I found Cosmo at a Jack Russell wirehaired terrier rescue facility in Orange County. He used to do on-lead agility competitions, a sport unique to Jack Russells. I loved his round, black eyes and expressive ears. Unusual for the breed, he had long, completely white hair.

Cosmo immediately came forward to meet me with tail wagging and showing his friendly, sweet nature. Right away, I was attracted to this cute and outgoing dog. I knew he had one of the major requirements for being an animal actor — he wasn't at all shy.

I never raise my actor dogs as puppies. Instead, I adopt them, usually at about one year old, from shelters or rescue groups. Since Cosmo was four or five years old when I adopted him, he may have been at the end of his agility career and wound up with a rescue group. I don't care about the past or analyze the details of the dogs I rescue. I accept them as they are today and move on into their future with me.

There are two most important and emotionally intense days for an actor dog and me. The first day is when the dog comes home with me. On adoption day, I take an animal's life in my hands. It's a huge responsibility. I promise to always do the right thing with him. We are embarking on this voyage together. Because we will be working in film, what we have done as a partnership will stay on file in history.

The second important and emotional time is the last day of a show in which the dog and I have gone through an incredible journey. We have accomplished contributing to a movie that will be on the screen forever as a classic American icon. That's the kind of experience I had with my Jack Russell terrier Moose when he played Eddie Crane on the television series *Frasier* for eleven years and old Skip in the movie *My Dog Skip*.

I wanted for Cosmo to be remembered in movies and television, too. But we had work to do.

From Paris to Pooches

In my birthplace of Paris, France, I raised and trained horses for jumping and dressage and worked with hunting dogs. I'd been around animals all my life. But nothing I did in Paris related to animal actor training. Still, I always had a kind of animal sense.

My experience training animal actors started simply. After I moved to Los Angeles, I wanted a permanent job and to stay in the United States. One day, I saw a cat food commercial on television. "Someone is telling the cat what to do," I thought. Although I didn't go to college or have any formal education that prepared me for this specialized work, the idea came to mind that I could possibly become a trainer working behind the scenes with animal actors.

I went to see a lot of animal movies and wrote down the names of head trainers. I contacted them about jobs with their companies. They all rejected me. Mostly, the companies were family businesses and didn't need to hire extra help. But I insisted, persuaded, and offered to volunteer. Eventually, Gary Gero, owner of Birds and Animals Unlimited, brought me into his company as a volunteer.

I started by cleaning cages and taking care of the animals. At that time, Birds and Animals Unlimited was small, with only a couple of dogs, cats, and bird actors. Gary participated in a live animal show at Universal Studios Hollywood. I

"It was so good to have American Humane Association on set making sure everything was done safely."

– **Jennifer Aniston**, actor, *Marley & Me*

worked there for a while — washing, feeding, cleaning the dogs, and helping out in general. Eventually, Gary hired me. Although I started by training dogs, I also trained many other types of animals, including birds, cats, and domesticated pigs.

During my volunteer days, I halfheartedly observed other animal trainers. It seemed to me that I could be successful if I used some of what I saw them do but also created my own style and techniques. One of my specialties turned out to be training dogs for character-driven stories in which the dog's role requires reacting or showing feelings rather than only doing tricks. In a horror movie, for example, a dog, as a character, may need to lower his head to show the emotion of fear.

Marley & Me

An effective animal-actor trainer must become expert at casting the right dog for the character he or she will portray. When I worked as lead animal trainer on *Marley & Me*, I chose Clyde, an overzealous yellow Labrador retriever — not in spite of his nature, but because of it. I look for dogs who have a variety of demeanors and attitudes that reveal their personalities. By choosing the right animal, I never have to stop the dog from being a dog and doing what is in his nature. Instead, I use what the dog brings. Clyde, like Marley, was not perfect, which made him the perfect dog for the role of the lovable dog who destroyed the Grogans' happy home.

To prepare Clyde for his role as "bad dog," I made our sessions into training games. Because I can't be visible in scenes, I placed pieces of hot dog where I wanted Clyde to go and then took the food away. The remaining scent made the dog gravitate to those spots. To encourage Clyde to tear up furniture and jump on people, I hid toys and tennis balls in cushions or strategically placed items of doggy interest in people's shirts and then said, "Go get it, Clyde." To make it easier for Clyde to stop doing a destructive behavior, I waited until the end of the day to do scenes in which the dog had to be more hyperactive. That way, he was physically less energetic. I also taught him the "stop" command. If a fully energized Marley had to be calmer for morning scenes, I removed all "dog-a-licious" scents from the set.

Evolving as a Trainer

While evolving my training techniques, I figured out that the most effective dog actors were not locked into the trainer all the time. So I developed an organic way of training. It gave the dogs confidence in their jobs while encouraging them to connect with actors on the film set and even at times when they were not working together. My philosophy is that the animal doesn't only relate to me personally. I use a less formal approach that gives the dog and me more freedom to adjust to each situation and for the dog to connect with other people. Once the animal is under control and we have a foundation for our work, I let go of him and deal with the moment. Flexibility and creativity have served me well. I never know exactly how I'm going to do something the director wants. Often, it's a last-minute decision. I must get into the situation or scene, assess it, and figure out what is required.

The animals have taught me how to train them. For example, Moose taught me to be versatile. Independent and intelligent, he was an incredibly challenging dog. He had no barriers when he decided he wanted to do or chase something. Being an animal actor gave this active dog a focus, a job to do that helped keep him happy and safe. After retiring from his work on *Frasier*, Moose lived with me for his remaining years, to the age of sixteen. When Kelsey Grammer accepted his 1994 Emmy for the show, he dedicated his award to Moose.

Cosmo's Natural Talents

As with Clyde and Moose, Cosmo's way of working is a natural fit for how I train animal actors. But soon after bringing Cosmo to his new home with me, I discovered things we needed to overcome. He would get nervous at times and lie flat on his belly. He'd look left and right as if to say, "Get me out of here." Then he'd run off. It took about two weeks for Cosmo to completely put behind him the animal shelter and wherever else he may have been. Drawing on my years of experience and the instantaneous love I felt for this cute dog, I was soon able to help him become more secure.

I want to portray relationships between an animal and a human actor that are genuine. Cosmo naturally loves people and relates to them in a spontaneous way without looking for the trainer to tell him what to do all the time. Quickly and fluidly, he connects with anybody around him. A spirited dog, Cosmo is motivated by treats, toys, and having the actor's attention during a rewarding playtime. He's extremely cuddly and affectionate. If someone talks to or kisses him, he wants to stay around and hang out with them. He's a happy little dog who loves to be part of whatever we are doing and likes to work, which is primary in all we do. Because of his natural curiosity, he thrives on the stimulation. He is confident and has complete trust in his surroundings and me.

As part of a dog actor's training, we rehearse with some distractions because movie sets have a lot going on. I like to train animal actors on the actual set and ask them to concentrate and focus. If something else is happening on set around him, Cosmo continues to tune in to me, his work, and the other actors. We spend time going over everything he is supposed to do for a scene. He stops working if he's not sure what to do.

When not at work, Cosmo enjoys being comfortable. Easy to live with, he is not at all obsessed with needing to stay active, although we like taking hikes together. He has a nice, soft bed at home, surrounded with his toys. A mellow dog, he sunbathes in the yard, yet he also hunts for his ball and toys and plays respectfully with my other dogs.

After spending so many years with Jack Russells, I've come to view Cosmo as my ultimate favorite. I've noticed that other people adore him, too. His versatility, intelligence, affectionate nature, and the sweet kindness in his eyes warm my heart all the time.

Cosmo and *Beginners*

Every skill I acquired through my years of experience blossomed while training Cosmo for the movie *Beginners*, written and directed by Mike Mills. In the film, Oliver (Ewan McGregor) is the son of Hal Fields (Christopher Plummer), who, at the age of seventy-five, reveals that he is gay and starts a relationship with a young boyfriend, Andy (Goran Visnjic). Arthur is Hal's dog, and Oliver inherits him when his father dies. The dog becomes the surviving connection between father and son. For his role in the movie, eighty-two-year-old actor Christopher won a Golden Globe, as well as Best Supporting Actor at the 84th Academy Awards.

When I met with Mike Mills, he told me he wasn't interested in using a dog actor who only did tricks for the trainer. He wanted a dog who was someone's pet, and then he'd have a trainer work with the animal. So I brought Cosmo with me to meet Mike and said, "Just play with him. I'll go elsewhere. See what he's like." They had a good time together. He appreciated that Cosmo was a friendly and lovable pet first and a dog actor second. Not too many directors will put their complete trust in an animal-actor trainer and let her direct the dog, but that's what it was like with Mike. After he saw me working with Cosmo, he put that aspect of the movie in my hands and let us do our work.

Ewan and Christopher were exceptional and embraced Cosmo in a touching way. Ewan loves dogs and was so eager to have a dog on set that working with him was a gift. He and Cosmo bonded quickly and had their own relationship. Ewan was willing to do whatever it took to work with Cosmo. When a human actor is cooperative to such an extent, he builds a relationship with the dog that becomes very special. Because of their bond, I could distance myself, which allowed Ewan and Cosmo to connect in real ways that could never be acted.

The love Ewan had for Cosmo was so strong that he wanted to know if I'd part with my dog. Of course, there was no way. After the film, Ewan adopted Sid, a rescue dog from an animal shelter who looked somewhat like Cosmo. Mike and Ewan still get together and often want to see Cosmo. They come by my house and take Cosmo for walks. I bring Cosmo to their houses, too. People who work with this dog tend to want to stay connected with him forever after.

Cosmo on a Movie Set

My job with Cosmo and other animal actors is to give them guidance and vision without them knowing it comes from me. They're not doing things because I said so. It's a partnership, not a relationship of a master and her dog. I talk to my animals on set with a low voice. I make myself not too present so I don't disturb the scene or actors. I remotely give cues the animals can see. When I have bigger dogs in a film, I use a louder voice. But in general, people can hardly hear me.

If there is something precarious on a movie set, it's up to me to deal with it in advance. I insist on only plastics, no breakables, so Cosmo and any other animals will not get hurt. I'm always aware of the surroundings.

Are there nails sticking out in the flooring? Are wires or other things loose that could cause accidents? I'm constantly exercising caution.

I never rehearse with the animals or bring them onto a set until I know how the actors are going to perform and what is going to happen in the scene. That way, I can prepare the animal for it. I find out if there is something that will need extra attention to keep the animal safe.

Most directors are respectful when I say I'm not comfortable with the way they want something done. Before production, we have meetings and talk things over. It's rare that someone insists on an action from the animal that might be harmful. If I don't want to do something I'm asked to do, I won't back off. The American Humane Association (AHA) certified animal safety representatives on the set have come to my aid three or four times. I have much respect for AHA.

If a director wants an animal to do something that might look crazy on film, we prepare for it in the safest ways, and I never do anything against the animal's will. By breaking the scene into small increments, I train slowly for actions that appear scary or dangerous, such as dogs hanging out of cars, jumping through windows, or crouching high up in trees. I videotape all my training and give it to the AHA safety representative on set for documentation.

Animal actor training is such a fun job. It has taken me to places I never thought I would go. No day is like another. No dog is the same as any other. I travel and train animals around the world and get to meet incredible people who are passionate about animals and committed to them. They are also the voice for animals and do everything possible to keep them safe.

Sometimes, animal actors get stereotyped as big stars in one role. Directors don't want to hire them because they're too popular and known for a certain part. Fortunately, Cosmo has also been cast in *Hotel for Dogs* and *Paul Blart: Mall Cop*. He has done commercials and auditioned for a television pilot. Because of his all-white fur, he has a lot of opportunities and is very versatile. We could put a black makeup patch around his eye, and he'd have a whole new look. Cosmo is about nine years old now. As far as his animal actor work goes, he's in his prime, and we have many more years ahead for us to work together creating memories in movies.

Tips for Training Dogs
from Mathilde de Cagny

Working with Moose's and Cosmo's individual talents showed me that if I went *with* an animal's natural flow and not *against* it, things worked out.

I like to compare training with cooking. It's like opening a refrigerator to see what's in it. Whatever is there, you make something out of it. You don't want to change the animal. You give him guidance and build trust. This makes the training organic, free, and spontaneous.

Cosmo's Acting Abilities

Ewan McGregor

It was wonderful working with Cosmo and Mathilde de Cagny in *Beginners*. Cosmo was very much a character in the movie.

I didn't often notice Mathilde doing her work, so it started to feel as if Cosmo was acting with me. Even when Mathilde couldn't be in the room, I still felt like he was acting with me.

There was one scene in which Cosmo surprised me. I showed him round my house, and Mathilde couldn't be in the room, since the camera was looking 360 degrees round the house.

As I pointed things out to Cosmo, he looked at them. I'd say, "This is the kitchen," and he'd look round the kitchen. "This is the living room," and he'd look round the living room. He was doing it all of his own accord. Mathilde wasn't there to show him what to do. He was looking at the rooms like he was really acting in the scene.

Ewan McGregor and Cosmo in *Beginners*

A movie set is a busy working environment. As an actor, I think it's very important that there are people on set whose job it is to look out for the welfare of the animals being used in movies. The animals' safety and comfort might otherwise be overlooked.

Since filming *Beginners*, Cosmo has remained a good friend of mine. I walk him now and then with Mathilde and my dog, Sid.

Blackie, Enzo, and Borsalino as Maximilian in *Hugo*
Worthy of a Golden Collar

Mathilde de Cagny

Except for a few background rodents in *Shutter Island*, acclaimed director Martin Scorsese had never worked with animal actors before he started filming *Hugo* in England. This movie would also be the first filming of live animals for 3-D, a process that required wide, complicated camera shots and moves. Timing was crucial in scenes with as many as three hundred extras milling around a busy train station, a variety of props, numerous background sounds, billowing smoke, and other sights and sounds that would distract and distress any dog.

From Estonia, England, and Germany, Blackie, Enzo, and Borsalino were selected to play the role of Maximilian (Max), the station inspector's (Sacha Baron Cohen) Doberman. The dogs were only one or two years old and had come to their first job with no previous movie experience. Blackie was the smartest and most courageous of the three Dobermans, in contrast to Enzo and Borsalino, who had big hearts but were not very brave. Enzo's greatest motivation was to play with his red ball. And Borsalino would do just about anything for my home-cooked food as his reward. The dogs' appearance — sleek black fur, pointy, standing-up ears, and gold-colored jowls — made them interchangeable for the camera.

When I received a call from Birds and Animals Unlimited in Los Angeles asking me to leave the country in a few days and become animal trainer for this complex movie that had already started shooting, I didn't think about all that would be involved. I was just thrilled to work for the legendary Mr. Scorsese and go to England.

I had to jump on a train after arriving in London and travel to where the film was being shot. Only two days had been allotted for me to get acquainted with the dogs and prepare them for their scenes. After I spent about twenty minutes on the set, I realized the level of expertise that would be required and how much responsibility lay on my shoulders. I had agreed to take on training dogs I didn't know, in a massive seventy-million-dollar movie, for a role that was integral to the plot and main characters. It would prove to be the most complicated and challenging film I'd ever done.

English dog trainers had spent two months preparing the three Dobermans and one month shooting the film. I met with the previous trainers to be briefed on their experiences so far. I needed to quickly observe and figure out the dogs' problems and how to solve them. Although Dobermans were originally bred and raised to be guard dogs, Blackie, Enzo, and Borsalino were not tough working canines who had reserves of bravery to call upon. On a movie set of this size, working with a crew and director who were unaccustomed to animal actors, they had become skittish. The dogs and I needed to rapidly build a trusting relationship in order to fulfill requests and overcome problems.

Blackie was the lead dog, and she played about 80 percent of Max's scenes. Enzo did most of the running and jumping up stairs. Each dog had to be trained the same way in case Blackie couldn't perform for some reason, such as in a scene that was too strenuous for one dog to repeat numerous takes or when it was necessary for two dogs to perform a chase scene.

Filming took place outside the United States, so American Humane Association (AHA) was not required to be on set. As a professional who had worked with AHA on films throughout my career, I had the experience and determination necessary to keep the animals safe. AHA safety representatives would have explained to the production crew or actors how to behave around the animals. The dogs had not been hurt, but they had become nervous when ignored and now were sensitive to being touched.

Meeting Mr. Scorsese

In addition to inserting myself into a production that had started before I arrived, I had to overcome the natural tendency to be starstruck. The set, almost a shrine-like atmosphere, was supposed to be quiet and focused at all times. No one talked directly to "Mr. Scorsese," who, as the saying goes, ran a tight ship. The people who worked for and revered him had each already won two or three Oscars. But none of them understood the process of training an animal for film.

The first time I met Martin, he laughed at my appearance. I was dressed as a 1930s man, in a mustache, wig, and hat, so I could stay near the dogs in crowd scenes. Ladies of that era wore long dresses, heels, gloves, and coats, which would make the physicality of my work impossible, and their clothing had no pockets where I could keep treats.

Mathilde de Cagny, in male period costume for *Hugo*, with Blackie

Martin showed interest as I explained the process and psychology of dog training for movies. He turned out to be a Francophile who liked that I was born and raised in Paris. We got along very well, and he appreciated everything we did. I resolved to call upon my years of animal-actor-training experience, put it out of my mind that I was working on a Martin Scorsese movie, and meet all the complex demands of the film.

Since the Dobermans were showing signs of anxiety, my first goal was to get them focused and confident. If they weren't comfortable, they couldn't think or stay in a good state of mind. I asked for twenty-five extras, a production assistant, and a camera operator who would become my personal crew and remain consistent throughout scenes in which the dogs played the role of Maximilian. My crew and I re-created a set that was identical to the environment the dogs would encounter with their first scene. That first day of rehearsal became a turning point. The dogs got their chance to do well — the key to any successful training process.

I taught the extras and crew how to respect the dogs' space by staying at least two feet away from them. When Maximilian was supposed to be lost in a crowd, I made sure heavy luggage did not touch the dogs from behind, which had previously made them jumpy.

Using a lot of toys for the dogs made their performances fun and effective. Each of the dogs liked to play with balls on strings. Enzo's attachment to a certain red tennis ball led me to tell everyone, "Don't lose that red ball." I often hid the dogs' favorite toys so they stayed focused on finding them and weren't distracted by everything that was going on around the set.

Most of Maximilian's scenes were with Sacha Baron Cohen, who was very businesslike and professional while rehearsing with the dogs. Although he was completely willing to spend the time necessary, he was involved in many other scenes. So we often worked with Sacha's stand-in to train the dogs. After *Hugo*, I worked for Sacha, training goats on his movie *The Dictator*.

After a couple of days of my working with them, the dogs changed. Almost as if by magic, they became calm and focused.

The Clock Tower Scene

One of the most challenging scenes was when Maximilian was supposed to search for the little boy, Hugo, who had been hiding in the train station's clock tower. To escape being found, Hugo has to crawl out onto the tower's enormous clock and cling to its hands. Maximilian was required to run up the stairs of the clock tower and search for Hugo in six or seven specific places, with the station inspector trailing behind him.

The camera was located at the top of the tower, where it filmed a 360-degree view of the building's all-glass frame. The tower's grate flooring had nowhere to hide toys or food. Instead of being able to stand nearby and instruct the dog, I had to stay out of camera range at the monitor with Martin. The dogs, mostly Blackie, would need to be so well prepared and programmed that they could perform this multilayered pattern of actions without me. I had only ten minutes to come up with a workable plan for accomplishing the difficult scene that appears effortless and fluid on-screen.

I dressed from head to toe in a green suit that would keep me invisible to the 3-D camera. My goal was to create surprising moments for Blackie before retreating to the monitor to watch the scene being shot. I placed and took away little pieces of hot dogs so Blackie would find the treats' lingering scents and get familiar with the area. I got down below the tower flooring and banged on parts of the scaffolding to entice Blackie to run and find toys I'd hidden in different places. But the scent of food and toys would only work for getting her to a few spots. How would I entice the dog to look as if she was trying to figure out where to run next?

To make it look natural for Blackie to investigate various spots in the clock tower, I hid three walkie-talkie radios in three locations and set them on three different channels. While my assistant trainer held the dog, to keep Blackie from hearing me, I went down to the monitor and stood far away from her.

As we had planned, Blackie found the hot-dog scents and ran to them. Then she looked around as if wondering, "Now what?" She started to turn, confused. I made a cat noise on one of the radios. "Meow!!" Blackie ran to the cat. Then I made a barking sound on the second radio. She rushed to the barking dog. I made another sound on the third radio. She hurried to see what was making that noise. Hearing intriguing sounds on the three radios made her appear to be thinking about her next moves and following Hugo's trail.

Ultimately, the camera had to follow Blackie from spot to spot and up, up, up the tower in one take. It took a week to shoot. In the final cut, the clock tower chase does not look as intense as when it was filmed, but everyone was pleased with how the scene turned out.

Martin and the Golden Collar Awards

Whenever Martin asked for last-minute things, he always told me to take my time. His level of support for working with the animals surprised and delighted me. Filming costs thousands of dollars per minute, and delays add to the expense. Still, he was patient while I figured out how to have the dogs give him what he requested.

In an op-ed piece for the *Los Angeles Times* and during a guest appearance on the *Ellen* show, Martin claimed to be "incensed" that Blackie had been snubbed for a Golden Collar Award. Martin professed his pride in a performance in which Blackie had risked losing audience sympathy by helping to find the little boy Hugo and evict him from the train station. Martin recalled the dog's bath scene with the station master, accentuating the profile of her regal nose, as a masterpiece for 3-D cinema. He defended the dogs against critics who assumed Blackie's acting had been enhanced by computer-generated imagery (CGI) and assured moviegoers that Blackie, Enzo, and Borsalino had done all their own stunts without any special effects.

Martin and Blackie appeared on a brief video clip at that year's Golden Collar Awards ceremony. In spite of the director's campaign, though, Uggie of *The Artist* won the 2012 Golden Collar Award. Later, I asked Martin for an endorsement of my work on *Hugo*. He wrote that I was not just a trainer but worked as part of a team by looking at all the details and what could be brought to the scene.

After the movie finished filming, Blackie, Enzo, Borsalino, and I did a fund-raiser for the Doberman Foundation in England. Blackie was so smart I wanted to take him home with me. The three Dobermans who were so memorable in the movie stayed in England and now make their homes with Birds and Animals Unlimited trainers there.

One of my dreams for the future is to be able to use all I have learned about finding dogs at shelters or through rescue groups, assessing their personalities and breed traits, and matching them to families, like mine, who will love them always.

Tips for Training Dogs
from Mathilde de Cagny

When a dog is misbehaving, use something that is more interesting and a stronger attraction to distract him.

Especially when you are walking a dog on his leash, you need to have control. You can use a clicker to let the dog know he's doing what you want, but I find that food works faster. Catch the moment when the dog is doing the desired behavior, and give him a positive reward. Ignore the negative behavior.

Chapter 13

SUE CHIPPERTON

(LOS ANGELES, CALIFORNIA)

Gidget

Gidget as the Taco Bell Dog
A Personality-Plus Chihuahua

Sue Chipperton

What can you say about a cute girl who got to spend quality time with Brad Pitt, Antonio Banderas, and other handsome film stars? You might call her lucky and talented. Or you might call her Gidget, a twelve-pound Chihuahua who came into my life as an eight-week-old, fawn-colored personality-plus puppy.

Over the years, I've worked with a variety of animals — dogs, cats, birds, rats, squirrels, even cockroaches — but my fondest memories on set are with Gidget, the Chihuahua who charmed the country in the late 1990s as the Taco Bell dog. She starred in a series of commercials that made her recognizable nationwide. When Gidget got cast for the Taco Bell commercial, no one knew the dog would become a pop-culture icon. Gidget charmed millions without ever saying a word and managed to make fast-food tacos adorable.

I met Gidget in 1995. I found her while casting puppies for a commercial. I was visiting the kennels of a Westie (West Highland white terrier) breeder in the Valley in Southern California. I suspected from the puppy's outgoing ways and high energy that she would make a good studio dog, or animal actor. When a trainer gets a new dog to train for studio work, whether a puppy or adult dog rescued from the pound, she can never be 100 percent certain if the dog will be a star. But a confident, outgoing, highly motivated dog with a great drive to play with toys is as good as it gets. At first glance, Gidget appeared to have all of those qualities.

Karin McElhatton, coowner of Studio Animal Services, where I work, approved of my bringing Gidget home to live with my Australian cattle dog, Beans, and me in my Venice Beach apartment. I was blessed with a landlord who looked the other way in regard to the building's no-pets policy.

While training Gidget, I soon discovered her love for tasty treats

— pieces of chicken, steak, and occasionally cheese — as motivators. She had a favorite stuffed toy called Mrs. Hedgehog. If I threw it on the ground between takes, she would chase and pick it up and then run back to her crate with it. At home, I could tell Gidget to get Mrs. Hedgehog out of her basket for a play session, and she would happily retrieve it from among all the other toys.

Becoming an Animal Trainer

The path that brought me to training animal actors and meeting Gidget started in my birthplace of England. My sister worked for the BBC, and I used to love accompanying her onto television sets. After I moved to the United States when I was nineteen, I wanted to train marine mammals. I was lucky enough to get a job at Ocean World in Fort Lauderdale, Florida, training dolphins, sea lions, and river otters. My coworkers told me that friends of theirs were hired by film studios to train animals. Until this point, I had never connected the two things that I enjoyed so much: going on film and television sets with my sister and my love for animals. It was like a lightbulb moment, when I realized I might be able to combine the two and actually get paid for it.

After looking further into the possibilities of becoming a studio-animal trainer, I realized that this was the type of work I wanted to do. I wouldn't be happy in an office and craved the variety of no two days ever being the same. So I packed up my things and drove cross-country to California. After a few false starts, I got into Studio Animal Services, beginning there as a volunteer. Karin gave me excellent on-the-job training. In what seemed like no time, I was going out on jobs as an assistant trainer. I have been with Studio Animal Services for close to twenty years now, training animals for movies, television, commercials, and print advertising projects.

The job has been a fascinating ride and fulfilled my wish for variety — no two days are the same. Early on, in downtown Los Angeles, I got to lie flat on my back in the pouring rain while Brad Pitt jumped between rooftops over my limp, wet, pathetic-looking body, as I released pigeons. Not quite how I imagined meeting a film star. It was during the filming of

Se7en that Brad's three large dogs got loose from his dog walker on the studio back lot and came charging over to check out Gidget. I wasn't sure of their intentions, but as I stood, pinned against a work truck, holding Gidget over my head and trying to protect her, Brad ran over to pull his dogs off me.

A National Dog Icon

On set, Gidget began to attract attention because of her work ethic. She loved going to a studio set and would light up, coming alive with eagerness and anticipation about going to work. She always knew the exact location of the camera. I'm sure she figured that the combination of camera and studio meant she would get her favorite treats. She walked onto the set; trotted across it ahead of me; wove through the legs of crew members; stepped up onto the riser; stood on her mark; and looked into the camera before I could even manage to get into position. People would be amazed to see her work with such precision and independence.

Gidget didn't do any tricks as the Taco Bell dog. Instead, she was successful because of her personality and ability to portray characteristics of what the company, at that time, considered to be their key demographic — eighteen- or nineteen-year-old college boys. With her confident, somewhat cocky attitude, her expressive eyes looked into the camera lens and connected with the company's most loyal customers. The people who worked around her on the commercials were always completely in awe.

Crew members who regularly work on feature films shoot commercials now and then to fill in between movies. Before he'd even seen Gidget, I overheard a seasoned and well-known director of photography (DP) complaining to his assistants. He didn't know that I was waiting with Gidget behind a screen before walking on set to work. He said, "This is going to be a long day, guys. Working with dogs is always difficult."

When it was our time to enter the set, Gidget trotted out and instantly landed on her mark. Her ears stood up straight. She looked perkily into the lens. After she nailed the shot, we walked back to her trailer. I heard the DP exclaim, "I've never seen anything like that!" He was completely blown away. Gidget had been ready and prepared. She knew exactly what she needed to do. Granted, she was never asked to do elaborate tricks, but she was a good worker and always a pro. The DP was converted into a Gidget fan.

And that was pretty much how it always went. Anybody new on a set or working with Gidget for the first time might be despondent, like that DP, about filming with a dog, but they walked away with a completely different view. Gidget loved working, and it showed.

A weird phenomenon began to occur after Gidget became famous. The whole time I was doing the Taco Bell campaign, people would come up to me and say, "My Chihuahua looks just like the Taco Bell dog." Then they would show me pictures of their dogs, and they didn't look anything like Gidget. Theirs could have been a black dog, a spotted dog, a dog with small ears, or a Chihuahua mix, but people were convinced they had Gidget's identical twin. I have yet to figure out the psychology of projecting her onto their pets.

Training and Protecting Gidget

In addition to training animals, it is also my job to protect them. It's not good to bring a tiny Chihuahua to a set where people are throwing things around and making loud noises — which is generally what happens on set before shooting starts. Because of all that commotion, the dog can get scared and never want to go back. It's my job to safeguard animals from that kind of experience. In the first year of the Taco Bell commercials, the client and the agency became very protective of this little dog. Under their instructions, when we walked on set, it was utterly quiet. In a perfect world, this level of silence would happen every time an animal is working on a set.

Preparing an animal on set is integral to making any scene work and having the dog feel comfortable. If both the trainer and the dog are prepared, the

> **DID YOU KNOW...?**
>
> In 1958, American Humane Association (AHA) began consultations with networks on the humane handling of animals for television productions. In 2009, the American Federation of Television and Radio Artists (AFTRA) awarded AHA its first grant from the AFTRA Industry Cooperative Fund.

team shows up on the day to shoot the scene, and there are no surprises. The dog knows what she's doing and what is expected of her.

One time, Gidget had to work in a taxicab. We did a shot of her sitting in the cab while I was on the street and another trainer crouched down on the car floor. Gidget wore a harness that ensured she couldn't jump out the window or off the seat. The remaining shots were done with the car on a gimbal — a big ball on which the car can move up and down without actually being driven. We had about a week of training time for Gidget to get used to being in a taxicab that rotated on a gimbal.

For another job, Gidget sat on a metal plate that was fixed to a little camera dolly crane. Computer-generated imagery (CGI) used a green screen to make it look as if she was sitting on Godzilla's tail. When they moved the crane up and down and back and forth, she was never higher than the height of my waist. Through prep and training prior to shooting, we achieved a level of comfort that made her look confident and alert for the scene.

A trainer must communicate with the crew prior to and during any shoot, but especially the kinds described above, when an animal is secured on a moving object. If something's not working right, I take the dog off the set and put her in her crate, usually in another room offstage where it's quiet. Then I come back and have a conversation with the director. Together, we figure out what can change and how to get a successful shot with the dog being comfortable. It's really important for a trainer to have those conversations and not just show up and put her dog in an uncomfortable situation.

Gidget's Acting Career

Whenever I am training dogs to do something new, I take them on set to my current job. This gets a dog used to set life, which generally consists of working for a while and then going back into her crate and sleeping. Taking the dogs to sets allows a new dog (or any animal) to get used to working in different environments with lots of scary-looking equipment and new people around. The dogs also figure out that crate time equates to their downtime. A seasoned studio dog will be asleep in her crate within five minutes of climbing in and lying down. Rest is a valuable commodity for a dog working on a feature film!

Tony Scott, with whom I'd often worked, saw me bring Gidget to the set one day when he was filming *The Fan*. He said, "Let's put her into this next scene." So she made a brief appearance in his film. That happened a lot with Tony. He loved his animals.

Gidget did a couple of scenes in *Legally Blonde 2: Red, White & Blonde*, where she played the mother of Bruiser, Reese Witherspoon's dog in the film. Bob Newhart worked with her in scenes, holding Gidget in his arms. The movie was fun for Gidget because she and Moonie, who played Bruiser, were already best friends in real life. In one scene, they were supposed to interact together, as if mother and son were being reunited after a long separation. Gidget and Moonie had been separated for a few days prior to shooting the scene. The end result on film was a natural, playful, and very cute interaction between the dogs.

Antonio Banderas directed *Crazy in Alabama*, a film in which Gidget had a small part working for another animal-training company, Birds and Animals Unlimited. Antonio commented that his children loved the Taco Bell dog. One time, he bent over and put his face close to Gidget's face and cooed baby talk to her. To my surprise, Gidget nipped his nose. I'd never seen her do anything like this before and was caught totally off guard. I was relieved when Antonio laughed and referred to it as a "love bite."

After that embarrassing situation, Gidget thought that nipping at someone's nose was a great game, especially if she was up high on a chair or tabletop. I started being more careful about watching her body language with new people and kept them from getting too close to her face.

Gidget's Farewell to Acting

Gidget's résumé included being a question in the Trivial Pursuit game and appearing in commercials for GEICO and Hardee's, but she was pretty much typecast as the Taco Bell dog. She didn't get much work after that campaign ended. When she was about ten years old, she retired to my home. She ran along the beach and played with my other dogs

— Beans, Hank (a blue Weimaraner), and Tula (a French bulldog). Over the years, Moonie remained her best pal and playmate, and they often visited with each other.

Although she had been in good health, on July 21, 2009, when she was fifteen years old, Gidget unexpectedly had a stroke. She died shortly afterward. She was an older dog, but I was still shocked. I am most grateful for the fact that I was home when it happened. It still haunts me today that if she had had the stroke while I was on set working, it might have been hours until I came home. I would have felt devastated if she had gone through this traumatic experience alone. Instead, I was able to hold Gidget and say good-bye.

Days later, after People.com posted a tribute to Gidget, reporters worldwide from newspapers, magazines, and TV shows called for interviews. Even though she hadn't been on television for several years, she was obviously still very much loved. The Associated Press picked up the story, and CNN, ABC, NBC, and all the other major news outlets ran stories about her life and death. She was mentioned on Letterman's and Leno's shows as well as *The View*. Bloggers posted tributes with their favorite memories of her. American Humane Association asked me to write an account of life with Gidget for one of their publications. In 2011, I cowrote a book about Gidget, with Rennie Dyball, called *A Famous Dog's Life*. Gidget's ashes, along with those of my other dog Beans, are sprinkled on their favorite beach in Malibu.

Tips for Training Small Dogs from Sue Chipperton

Each animal is different, with an individual personality. What works with one doesn't work with others. You have to be versatile and creative when training dogs, but most of all, patient. I've had dogs in the past who weren't food motivated, but they loved a tennis ball and would work for playtime with the ball. Respect the dog's individuality and find out what is a reward for him. Then use this reward for a positive training session.

Chapter 14

CHRISTINA POTTER

(NORTH BERGEN, NEW JERSEY)

Gable

Gable as Willie Nelson in *Our Idiot Brother*
From Agility Champion to Animal Actor

Christina Potter

When our golden retriever, Kelly, gave birth to her first and only litter of puppies, I named one of the pups Gable, after the actor Clark Gable. Little did I know at the time that, like his namesake, Gable would find acting in his future.

When Gable was eight weeks old, my husband, Taylor, and I started focusing Gable on positive-reinforcement training. He took to it easily. He retrieved toys and received treats for learning new skills. We made training sessions interactive, with fun games that get a dog's attention. Gable grew into a slender, healthy dog who didn't overeat, so food, in itself, didn't motivate him. His motivation was the positive reinforcement he received.

Although he ate anytime he was hungry, when we made food his training reward, it became part of the game. Whenever Gable saw me pull out the treat bag, he looked as if he was asking, "What do you want me to do now?" He even offered behaviors we had taught him, in hopes of getting a reward. A naturally happy and friendly dog, he mostly wanted to please us. He loved the attention, praise, and human interaction.

We taught Gable obedience commands, such as "sit," "stay," and "down." We added to his interest by introducing agility training. Agility is a performance sport in which you and your dog compete as a team at trials offered by different associations. I currently compete in American Kennel Club (AKC) agility with Hudson (Gable's son) and our two other dogs. Agility demonstrates the bond between handler and dog by showing the dog's willingness to run through an obstacle course directed by the handler. The obstacles must be performed correctly, in the numbered sequence and at a controlled high rate of speed. Obstacles include jumps, weaves, teeters, etc.

By 2001, when Gable was one year old, we were participating in

AKC competitive obedience events with him and Kelly. In competitive obedience, a dog must perform the commands given by the handler, as instructed by the judge. The commands can only be given once, either by hand signal or verbally. A dog must perform quickly and accurately. Gable excelled at both types of training. He had an impressive two AKC agility championships (Master Agility Champion and Preferred Agility Champion) — as well as an AKC competitive obedience title.

Discovering Animal Actors

Our household consisted of four other dogs of different breeds and sizes, cats, ferrets, and horses. Gable never showed aggression and was mellow with everyone. He and Kelly were so talented and loving that I wanted to share them with people who might need and appreciate a dog's comforting presence. I attended a seminar with the intention of having them become therapy dogs who would visit hospitals and schools. A speaker at the seminar talked about her dog, who was an animal actor.

After the seminar, I contacted an agent who finds jobs for animal actors and learned that the dogs needed trick training to get work in films and television. Tricks can include taking a bow, dancing, or barking on command. These tricks must be performed reliably, at a distance, and sometimes only with visual commands. I started teaching tricks to Gable and Kelly right away.

I also contacted All Star Animals and Animals for Advertising, two premier animal talent agencies in New York. I asked about their trick-training requirements and the possibility of jobs for Gable and Kelly as animal actors. The companies put Taylor and me on their call lists, and we started going out on assignments. Gable did commercials, catalogs, infomercials, print ads, store-window display shoots, and modeling for calendars. *Saturday Night*

> **DID YOU KNOW...?**
>
> Professional trainers say that most producers and directors recognize overtly unhappy, stressed-out, and fearful animals or unsavory and unscrupulous trainers. They don't want them on their projects. The film industry is a small world. Word travels about which trainers are skilled and careful.

Kelly on an agility course

Live (*SNL*) and *Late Night with Conan O'Brien* featured him in skits. Always easygoing yet showing a strong work ethic, Gable understood the difference between work and play. If a camera was nearby, he'd look into it. Gable's son, Hudson, also worked as an animal actor. He played the dog on top of Mitt Romney's car in an *SNL* spoof about the presidential candidate traveling cross-country on a family vacation.

As Gable, Kelly, Hudson, and I gained more experience, I came to the conclusion that animals don't act. Dogs are just too honest about their emotions to have pretense. They're doing actions they've been trained to do. They know that if they do this action, they'll get this reward, and it's really good. If the dogs don't want to be animal actors and it isn't any fun for them, they just don't do what the trainer asks. You can't force them. I had an Afghan hound who would rarely do a trick if I asked her. Even though I've trained dogs for twenty years, she wouldn't respond. That was fine. She had a very lovely life and did some agility competitions and rallies.

It's a misconception about animal actors to think, "This poor dog is working so hard." For them, it's fun, an adventure, a chance to meet new people, and very stimulating to the senses. When dogs are in a movie or other media, it's because they want to do it. When we are on a set, if I say the dog needs a break, everything halts, and the dog takes a break. I take crates to work so the dogs have a place to relax. Between takes, they are outside walking, getting water, playing, or sleeping in their crates.

Gable's Starring Role

When Gable was ten years old, he won a pivotal role in the comedy *Our Idiot Brother*. In the movie, Ned (Paul Rudd) serves a jail sentence and then tries to return to his idyllic life on an organic farm with his girlfriend, Janet (Kathryn Hahn), and their dog, Willie Nelson. Huggable Gable was a favorite of Paul Rudd, who used to have a golden retriever. He and Kathryn Hahn were kind, attentive, and positive to the dog.

Near the end of filming the movie, Gable ran an agility course during his time off set and was his usual energetic self. But later that week, I noticed that my ordinarily happy, active dog suddenly didn't want to retrieve or play anymore. Believing something was wrong, I took Gable to the veterinarian three times in one week and was assured that the dog was merely aging. His mother, Kelly, was still active at age thirteen, so I didn't believe that aging was a good explanation for his lethargy. I also knew that golden retrievers are good at hiding their pain until it's unbearable.

I left Gable with the vet so he could run some tests. He called me while I was on the movie set, with the news that Gable had cancer. He wanted to do surgery right away. Taylor and I agreed to the surgery. Gable lived for only five hours after the surgery.

Gable's death came as a shock to us. He had not shown signs of being terminally ill. Taylor and I were heartbroken. We had lost an irreplaceable and patient family member who had taught us so much about everything and introduced us to a world of canine performance sports that continues to be our passion. He was there for us, in good times and in bad. To this day, it is difficult to speak of his loss without crying.

When Gable died, I wasn't the only one who cried. The director, Jesse Peretz, was such a nice guy. He called a break for the evening and said, "We understand." He made me feel that they weren't only about the movie and the money. The cast and crew were very empathetic about our loss. I found comfort with Judy Johns, American Humane Association's certified safety rep. She is the most compassionate person I've ever met. The support she gave me when Gable died was unbelievable.

Many of the scenes Gable was supposed to be in had been filmed in the days before he died. Kelly and Hudson finished the film by alternating in the role of Willie Nelson. At the end of filming, Paul Rudd said, "When the movie comes out, it's going to be difficult. But instead of being sad, think of it as a beautiful tribute."

Gable died in August 2010, and Taylor and I, who had both been on-set trainers, saw the film in December. Watching the film was bittersweet indeed. We enjoyed the beautiful memories of those last days with Gable but mourned his loss. The hole in our hearts was as big as it had been the day he died. As we watched, we comforted each other by holding hands. Words could not be spoken. For a long time, I couldn't bear to talk about Gable or his untimely death.

Kelly died in April 2013, at the age of sixteen. Hudson still goes up for parts that call for golden retrievers. I continue working with our other animal actor dogs, Morgan, a Chinese crested, and Chester, a Berger Picard. Like Gable, they bring smiles to the faces of people who see them in commercials and films. Losing Gable taught me that life with our pets is never long enough. We must cherish every moment, enjoy every opportunity to spend time with them. By giving our pets a stimulating life with a challenging environment, we can make sure they have the opportunity to flourish and be happy.

Tips for Training Dogs from Christina Potter

Always set your dog up for success. When teaching any new skill, start in a very quiet environment in which your dog is comfortable. The familiarity of your home will allow your dog to concentrate on you. Once you've mastered that, move to a different, but still quiet, location.

If you move too quickly and your dog fails, go back to where he or she was successful and reinforce that. It is important to never set your dog up for failure, as this will only frustrate both you and the dog. Finish each exercise on a positive note.

Always work in small steps, giving your dog the best opportunity to succeed. Remember, your dogs are working with you because they want to make you happy. Shouldn't you want the same for them?

Chapter 15

STEVE BERENS
(ACTON, CALIFORNIA)

Abbey in her backyard

Abbey as Sam in *I Am Legend*
Will Smith's Canine Costar

Steve Berens

In the 2007 movie *I Am Legend*, military virologist Lieutenant Colonel Robert Neville (Will Smith) is one of the few people immune to a genetically engineered virus that killed 90 percent of humanity. Vampire-like creatures prey on the earth's survivors. Grieving for his wife and daughter, Robert lives a solitary existence with his faithful companion, a German shepherd named Sam (Samantha), while he attempts to find a cure for the virus. *I Am Legend* became a hit film and so did its canine costar, Sam.

Francis Lawrence, the film's director, called to ask if I could train a female dog for the role of Sam. Most available German shepherd movie animals are tough-looking males with the dark coloring that is a trait of the breed. Francis wanted an American German shepherd with a lighter-colored face and light eyes. Normally, I'd spend a couple of weeks before making a decision about whether I can work with a dog and if she is the right choice for an important role. But this movie would begin shooting in Manhattan at the end of September, and I only had three months to train the dog for a first acting job.

> **DID YOU KNOW...?**
>
> In 2009, American Humane Association did a major update of its *Guidelines* and increased the user-friendly manual to 128 pages, including humane treatment guidelines for animals in rodeos, camera cars, and reality television.

In mid-July, I found Abbey at a German shepherd kennel in central California. She was about two years old. I visited her a couple of times and could tell that she had a nice attitude. Abbey was a very personable dog. She retrieved balls as often as I would throw them for her but was not so compelled to instinctively chase as to make her unreliable. Her sweet temperament, prey drive, and fondness for people were characteristics that made me think, "This could work." They also gave me keys I needed to quickly figure out what would motivate her. Relying on over thirty years of experience as an animal trainer, I sensed that she'd be a good choice for the role of Sam.

Training Abbey and Her Doubles

Although a completely untrained dog, Abbey was a fast learner, which showed her intelligence. Still, it was challenging to prepare her in the amount of time we had before shooting started.

We built our relationship by playing ball together, going for walks, and just spending time as companions. Abbey tried hard to learn everything she was supposed to do and was happy working. She concentrated well and stayed focused. She responded to my positive-reinforcement type of training like a child doing well in class because she loves her teacher.

To serve as a backup for Abbey, I found another German shepherd in a shelter. I rescued her and called her Sammy. I intended for Sammy to do more aggressive work for the film. Another dog named Kona came from a German shepherd breeder. Kona would step in when Abbey needed to rest. On set, Sammy and Kona got makeup on them to lighten some of the darkness on their faces so they would more closely resemble Abbey, with her light eyes and face.

It worked out that we used Kona for only one shot — to chase the ball a few times on a flat barge when Abbey was too tired. Sammy did an aggressive snarling shot that didn't make it into the movie. Abbey provided everything else.

From Animal-Loving Kid to Animal Trainer

In challenging situations, such as selecting and preparing dogs quickly for a movie role, I've had to call upon all I've learned about training. I have always loved animals. When there was a stray dog in the neighborhood, I was the kid who kept the dog safely in our family's garage until I found the owner.

My uncle was legendary Hollywood animal trainer Ray Berwick.

He trained the birds on Alfred Hitchcock's *The Birds* in the early era of animals in film. When I was in college and feeling directionless after my father's passing, I visited my uncle in Los Angeles and discovered how much I liked training animals for movies. While I was still in school, I worked at Sea World. After I graduated, Uncle Ray brought me into animal actor training as an apprentice cleaning cages. He gave me the opportunity to follow him into the business. I jumped on it and never looked back.

At first, I read every book I could find on the subject of training animals for films. Fortunately, I learned the "handed-down art" from people who knew what they were doing. The best and most successful trainers showed me that positive reinforcement makes the whole thing work. They taught me that it's all about the relationship.

In 1986, I started Steve Berens' Animals of Distinction with my wife, Tina Berens. It is my honor to carry on the line of professional trainers that runs from my uncle Ray to me. Animal training has led to some exciting encounters with world-famous actors, like Will Smith.

Abbey and Will Smith

I took Abbey to meet Will Smith in Los Angeles prior to their working together in New York, so he and the dog could get to know each other. On their first visit, she barked as if telling him that he would have to win her respect. We scheduled hour-long sessions three times a week. Will came to our training sessions with an attitude of wanting to work with the dog, which makes the whole experience much easier.

Even though Abbey had to look to me for her direction, she and Will needed to interact with each other during their many scenes together. Abbey would heel as she walked alongside Will, and he gave her food treats that I provided, so their bond could develop into a natural relationship. When she watched Will, she got a treat. The result of our training sessions was that Abbey took my cues but it never seemed that she was relying on me. She looked every bit the part of Will's dog. The genuine relationship between Will and Abbey became a highlight of the filming experience.

Sometimes, an actor comes to a shoot with the preconceived idea that he doesn't want to work with a dog. He might think the dog is going to steal scenes and attention from him. If you get in a situation where the actor doesn't want anything to do with the dog but you have to make the shots succeed, the actor becomes like a prop that we work around. Will couldn't have been easier to work with or more helpful. If he noticed any frustration over getting a shot, he would come over and ask, "What can I do to help this out?"

If actors are willing to work with the dog and view the animal as another actor, because that's what the dog is, it looks much better on film. That's the kind of communication I also had on *The Mask* with Jim Carrey and a little Jack Russell terrier named Max.

Abbey after the Movie

After six months of filming, the crew had fallen in love with Abbey, and she loved them. She really pulled off those shots with Will, and their scenes did not take a long time. The crew appreciated and loved Abbey,

Abbey,
Will Smith's infatuation

but production also respected her as a contributing cast member. Francis and the crew petted and congratulated Abbey when she finished her last scene.

In a press conference for the movie, Will talked about Abbey's ability to recognize the cue "rolling" and, on hearing it, run to get on her mark. He commented that Abbey seemed to sense, and even empathize, when things weren't going well for him in a scene. At the end of their time filming together, Will jokingly asked me to let him have Abbey in exchange for a house in the hills. I replied, "Abbey has her own family. But she can come by for sleepovers anytime." Will referred to his infatuation with Abbey as a fleeting Hollywood romance.

Although Abbey is our family pet, she continues to do some commercial work and was involved with the Christian Slater television series *Breaking In*. It doesn't matter to me whether she works again or not. Abbey lives in our house and backyard. She raised our bulldog, Sarge, who tries to keep up with her by playing keep-away games with the ball. Abbey gets along with our cats, dogs, and children. She is calm and agreeable with any other animals who live with us while I am doing projects with them.

Abbey really only has one flaw: she kisses too much. I have to tell her, "Not everybody wants five kisses when they first meet you."

Tips for Training Dogs
from Steve Berens

Positive reinforcement makes the whole thing work. Listen to the animal and don't be too stringent in trying to make everything fit your way.

Evaluate the animal and what it will take to move him forward, because each one is different. Even in a litter of dogs, they all have totally different attitudes.

A lot of people want to know the secret to training a dog. Food? No, it's the companionship.

Chapter 16

KAREN ROSA

(LOS ANGELES, CALIFORNIA)

Frank Inn and Benji (Higgins)

Higgins as Benji, and Frank Inn,
the Father of Humane Training
Inspiring a Million Shelter-Pet Adoptions

Karen Rosa

The power of casting animals in movie roles as a force for positive change has never been more fully realized than when a fluffy rescued
dog named Higgins met a walking miracle named Frank Inn. Higgins,
the huggable dog who originated the role of Benji, and his affable trainer,
Frank Inn, known as the Father of Humane Training, inspired a million adoptions of animals from shelters. Because of Frank's example and
success with Benji, about 70 percent of the dogs in Hollywood film and
television productions are rescued and introduced to new lives as animal
actors. Together, Frank Inn, Higgins, and Joe Camp, through the Benji
series, transformed the image of "mutts" from undesirables into cool
companions and family pets.

In 1998, I had the privilege of interviewing Frank, who by then was
acknowledged as one of the world's leading animal trainers. I was pro-
ducing the tribute to him given by American Humane Association (AHA)
at the Disneyland Hotel in Anaheim that year. I looked forward to meeting the smiling, big man with a white, curling mustache who always wore
a sea captain's hat.

With good reason, I felt in awe of this large man with the infectious
smile. By then, Frank had won forty Picture Animal Top Star of the Year
(PATSY) Awards from our organization and had been inducted into the
AHA Hall of Fame. Higgins and his offspring, who played Benji after the
first movie, had twice won the American Guild of Variety Artists Georgie
Award for Top Animal Entertainer of the Year. Benji was voted one of
the top ten most popular performers in the United States in a Performer
Q survey. Seventy-one million people had watched the Benji films in theaters. A billion people worldwide had seen Benji on television.

Frank Inn's Journey to Fame

Frank was born on May 8, 1916, in Camby, Indiana, and named Elias Franklin Freeman. The son of a strict Quaker preacher, Frank lived with his family in a tent that served as parsonage for the church his father built from the wreckage of an abandoned sawmill. At age seventeen, Frank decided he wanted a career in movies. He hitchhiked to California and changed his name to Frank Inn. His first job was as a horse-stable boy. Soon, MGM hired him to do janitorial and maintenance work at its studio, where he made $29.50 a week.

Frank seemed to never tire of telling the story of how close he came to death in the mid-1930s, when he was nineteen years old. A drunken driver in Culver City slammed into him while Frank was walking down the street. Frank was pronounced dead and taken to the morgue. That day, students from a morticians' school were there to learn embalming techniques, but their instructor was late for class. While they waited, one student detected a heartbeat in Frank's body and called out, "He's not dead." Frank was rushed to the hospital for surgery.

For the next two years, Frank was confined to a wheelchair. Because he was destitute and had astronomical hospital bills to pay, Frank's friend

Karen Rosa and
her dog Susie

Art Close brought the young man home to live with his family. Shortly before Frank's arrival, a stray dog had wandered into the Close family's home and promptly birthed a litter. Art found homes for all but one pup, who happened to be his son Bobbie's favorite. Bobbie devised a plan for convincing his dad to let him keep the puppy. He asked Frank to say that while the family was at work and school, Frank got lonely and needed relief from the constant boredom. The puppy would provide companionship.

Bobbie's plan succeeded. The family named the puppy after the cartoon character Jeep. Because Jeep needed house training, Frank devised a method of luring him to a doggy door by placing thin slices of sausage along its edges. Even with Frank still in a wheelchair, and never having trained a dog, he taught Jeep to bark when he raised his hand. He spent long hours, sitting in a wheelchair, amusing himself and the dog by teaching Jeep more tricks.

When Frank returned to MGM in 1934, he swept the floors and had wages garnished by fifteen dollars a week to pay his medical bills. At the time, Henry East was training Skippy, the dog who played Asta for the *Thin Man* series of movies. One day, Henry was having trouble getting the dog to climb stairs, get into bed, stick his head out, and bark. Frank watched the troubled training session and said, "My dog can do that." He went home, brought Jeep back to the studio, and showed Henry that Jeep could live up to Frank's claims. He explained that Jeep could also act out retrieving a ball. "Speak," Frank ordered. Jeep barked. Henry said, "You got the job," and asked Frank to work with him on the *Thin Man* series.

As his reputation for outstanding results grew, Frank continued working as an animal trainer on films. He trained Gene Autry's dog, Rebel, and Roy Rogers's Bullet. By 1943, Frank was assisting Rudd Weatherwax in training Pal, the first Lassie. For thirteen years, he continued to work with the collies who played the Lassie character in films.

In 1951, Frank went into business for himself. He pioneered the use of conditioned response — a reward-based system that started with giving an animal food (biscuits or meat) and used a clicker to let the animal know when he'd done something right. Trainers and assistants learned from Frank's hallmark ability and conviction that it was necessary and humane to train animals with kindness and love. Frank could train just about any animal — chimpanzees, elephants, birds, chickens. Once, he designed a swimming race between a cat and a chicken. He liked to say, "We can teach them anything." One of the animal actors he trained during the middle of his career was Orangey, who played Rhubarb — a cat who owned a baseball team. Orangey lived to be twenty-three and worked in more than five hundred films. Frank also trained Bernadette, the basset hound who played Cleopatra (Cleo) in the Jackie Cooper TV series *The People's Choice*. The characters of Rhubarb and Cleo brought Frank his first two PATSY Awards.

During his years as a prominent Hollywood trainer, Frank forged a lasting and mutually satisfying relationship with American Humane Association (AHA). He said that the certified animal safety representatives would call him at night to find out where he and his assistants would be working the next day. If Frank told them that the studio had requested something that worried him, the AHA representative made sure he didn't have to fulfill the request if it was wrong for the animals.

Enter Higgins

In 1960, an animal control officer from Burbank Animal Shelter called Frank and said, "There's a real cute puppy here. You've got to see him." The dog needed a home; he would be euthanized if no one adopted him. Frank went to meet the fluffy, honey-brown mutt with expressive brown eyes. The distinctive-looking dog — a cross between a miniature poodle, cocker spaniel, and small terrier or schnauzer — won Frank's heart. He adopted Higgins and brought the dog home to start a life that neither of them could have imagined at the time.

Frank recounted that he started training Higgins by combining work and play. The dog was fond of running alongside his motorcycle. He and his wife, Juanita, took Higgins with them on camping and fishing trips. Higgins, eager to join in the fun, would jump into their boat. Demonstrating his intelligence and creativity, Higgins taught himself to pull up the fishing wire until a fish landed in the boat.

While Frank continued to train Higgins at home, he worked with

Orangey in *Breakfast at Tiffany's* and *Cat on a Hot Tin Roof.* Fairchild, the bear in *Daniel Boone*, became another of Frank's many memorable animal actors. Then along came a television series that captured the country's imagination with its humorous return to simpler times — *Green Acres*. For this show, Frank trained Arnold Ziffel the pig, and won his third PATSY. Arnold amused audiences with such accomplishments as opening mailboxes and doors, pulling a wagon around the yard, and watching himself on television. Arnold earned $7.43 an hour for snorting through an eight-hour day.

In 1964, Frank was finishing up nine years of training four hundred animals, including Elly May Clampett's menagerie for the *Beverly Hillbillies* series. He heard that an upcoming television show called *Petticoat Junction* needed a dog character. He told the producer about Higgins and brought the dog in for an audition. During Higgins's seven seasons with the show, critics called the dog the best actor in the cast. Frank noted that Higgins had to master one trick per show for thirty-nine shows a year.

The stint on *Petticoat Junction* was more than enough for one little shelter dog who, like Frank, had been plucked from the jaws of death. Frank retired Higgins at the age of thirteen, even though the dog was in perfect health. He believed that working dogs are happier and live longer lives. But Higgins had had a great career that Frank assumed was over. The dog would spend the rest of his days eating beef and biscuits.

> ### DID YOU KNOW...?
>
> In 1951, AHA created a stamp of approval for movies that committed to humane practices while filming animals.
>
> Also in 1951, Ronald Reagan hosted the first PATSY Awards, to honor outstanding animal actors. Jimmy Stewart presented an award to Molly for her work as Francis the Talking Mule.

Along Came Joe Camp

In 1973, producer and director Joe Camp wanted to film a movie the likes of which had never been done. He wanted the star dog in his movie to act, not merely do tricks or perform what he had been trained to do. When

Joe visited Frank's ranch, he explained that the dog of his dreams would visually express happiness, sadness, curiosity, focus, and honesty. There would be no cutaways or assembling the dog's actions through editing. Instead, the film would use long master shots with a camera following the dog continuously from one place to another and recording his point of view. Joe wanted audiences to be able to understand what the dog was thinking. The dialogue would literally be in the eyes of the dog.

Joe had extensively visited animal trainers and animal shelters but hadn't found his ideal canine. Frank showed him all that Higgins could do. Joe was mesmerized and instantly decided to cast Higgins. As Joe looked for the dog who would play Benji's girlfriend, Frank showed Joe every dog in the place except for Tiffany, a white Maltese, who was in sick bay with a minor ailment. Joe saw Tiffany through a door and went in to get a closer look at her. He decided Tiffany would be Benji's love interest in the movie. In the film clip we showed at the AHA tribute to Frank and Benji, Frank said, "It took everything I've ever known to pull it off, but we did it. This was the first live-action animal picture to get the same emotional involvement and response that Disney has always gotten with animated pictures."

Higgins impressed Joe by never looking at the trainer off camera, but only at the spot he was supposed to be watching within the scene. Frank, Higgins, and Joe did a cross-country tour that gathered crowds of joyful children and adults who adored the winsome dog. In a letter to Frank, Joe wrote, "I would never admit it at the time, but most of the things that you said were impossible really were impossible, but somehow you always found a way.... There has never been anything like it on the screen before."

Critics agreed. They called Benji a remarkable performer who could act with energy and showed incredibly deep characterization in his roles. The critics raved that the dog communicated, sustained a mood, and displayed exceptional acting ability. He expressed anger, fear, love, happiness — a complete range of emotions that equaled that of renowned human actors. They heralded Benji as one of the most accomplished canine actors in America, on a par with or even surpassing Lassie, Rin Tin Tin, and Old Yeller in talent and charisma.

By the time the first Benji movie was filmed and promoted, Higgins was seventeen and had been working for fifteen years. It really was time for him to lie in the sun and retire after an even greater blaze of glory. The next three Benji movies starred Higgins's daughter, Benjine, who also appeared in Benji television specials. She immediately became Benji and was never called Benjine again. There was a bit of gender confusion going on, since the new Benji was a girl. Frank referred to her as both "he" and "she" while he trained or talked about her. She even learned to lift one leg, like a little boy dog, to relieve herself.

The new Benji could do anything Frank asked of her. In a gentle voice, he repeatedly gave her verbal commands and used hand gestures to get her to do behaviors such as yawn, sneeze, shake her head, and point with her right foot. He rewarded her with little cubes of steak that he kept in his pockets. To demonstrate the dog's mastery of human vocabulary, he would ask her to pick up an object by name, then put a blindfold on her to show that she wasn't relying on watching his signals to identify which object to select.

Like her father, the new Benji accompanied Frank and Joe on U.S. and world tours. It was astonishing to see how calm the dog remained as excited children grabbed at her, clutched her nose and ears, and held her head in their tiny hands. By the time Benji was featured on the cover of *TV Guide*, the character was one of the most popular animals in the history of movies. Accolades were even garnered by other aspects of the Benji movies. In 1974, the theme song, "I Feel Love," received an Academy Award nomination and won a Golden Globe.

In late 1975, Higgins died, at the age of seventeen. Frank had the dog's ashes put into an urn. He kept the urn with the Benji memorabilia stored in a special room he had built onto his house.

Joe Camp began the search for Benji number three in 2001 to star in the fifth Benji movie. Joe's visits to animal shelters around the country, appearances on national television and news programs, and promotion of *Benji: Off the Leash!*, in which Benji saves his mother from a backyard puppy mill, generated more than one billion media exposures for shelters, adoption efforts, and animal rescue groups. Joe gathered together all of Benji's movies and videos. He hoped that children, parents, and teachers would view and discuss Benji- and Higgins-related messages about succeeding in life even when it looks as if you don't have a chance. The Benji collection presents themes of love, hope, persistence toward a goal, and never giving up. People can view the Benji website at www.benji.com. For more of Frank Inn's personal story, see *Joe Camp's The Phenomenon of Benji* by Frank Inn.

Frank Inn's Legacy

At the height of his long career, Frank was considered to be the best animal trainer in the industry. He cared for a thousand animals — dogs, cats, farm animals, and wildlife — on his industrial-zoned Sun Valley ranch. Because he couldn't bear to see healthy animals euthanized, he continued to adopt the unfortunate ones from animal shelters. If they had acting ability, he and assistants trained them to be animal actors. If they weren't suited to that type of work or lifestyle, he placed the rescued animals in good homes where they could be family pets. He also retired animals on his ranch who had worked with him and his trainers. These included Arnold the pig, who grew to a hefty six hundred pounds, making him too big to perform on *Green Acres*. Frank called Arnold "the retired ham." With all these adopted, retired, and working animals, Frank said that his ranch's feeding bills came to four hundred dollars per day.

Thanks to Frank, millions of people, who'd seen the many animals he'd trained for film and television, got the message that animals from shelters make fantastic pets. As part of our tribute to Frank, AHA donated a special portrait of Benji for display at the Burbank Animal Shelter, where Frank had found Higgins. AHA tried to get Frank a star on the Hollywood Walk of Fame. The committee rejected the request. But Benji's paw prints are part of the Burbank shelter's TV and Movie Animal Walk of Fame. Later, Joe Camp continued the tradition of Benji as a model for pet adoption. He partnered Benji with Pets911.com to promote shelter pets who need homes.

Frank hired as many as thirty trainers and handlers and brought a whole new generation trained in his humane methods to Hollywood. He taught trainers to communicate with animals and respect their intelligence instead of only viewing them as capable of performing tricks. Karl Lewis Miller, trainer for the animals in the *Babe* movies and a dear friend of Frank's, was one of his most famous protégés.

Frank's wife, Juanita, to whom he had been married for fifty years and who worked with him training animals, died in 1996. After her death, Frank retired. He enjoyed writing poetry and spent a lot of time doing things for his church, such as donating a van to give elderly people rides to church. Frank never tired of helping charities, and he promoted humane animal training. He worked with Toys for Tots, the Muscular Dystrophy Association, and organizations that provide service dogs for people with disabilities. He contributed to Starlight Children's Foundation, SOS Children's Villages–USA, Actors and Others for Animals, the Animal Humane Society of Hennepin County, Minnesota, and shelter-pet adoption organizations across the country.

Just as Frank had started animal training while sitting in a wheelchair during recovery from his near-fatal accident, he lived out his retirement riding in an electric golf cart. He occupied his time by assembling and tending to a museum of memorabilia that included awards and photos of him posing with Hollywood stars, such as Cary Grant, Bing Crosby, Natalie Wood, Frank Sinatra, Dean Martin, and Ronald Reagan. Frank's Benji room housed plush toys, puppets, puzzles, Benji books, and just about any other kind of Benji-related item. He stored in engraved urns and wooden chests the ashes of animals he had trained.

Frank died of diabetes at age eighty-six on July 27, 2002. He told his children that he wanted Higgins and other animals he had trained to have their ashes buried in his casket inside special pockets. By the time of his death, though, California law wouldn't allow this type of arrangement. Frank was buried in Hollywood Hills. His daughter Kathleen Copson kept the remains of Higgins, Arnold, Tramp (from *My Three Sons*), and other animals her father had trained.

Frank was a wonderful man. He was an inspired trainer — and an inspiration to me and all the trainers who use the humane methods he pioneered. Although today we have many technological advancements that help filmmakers depict complicated animal action, such as sophisticated animatronics and computer-generated imagery (CGI), Frank and Benji proved that there is nothing like the real thing. Frank's compassionate training and the bond it created truly brought magic to the screen.

Tips for Training Dogs from Frank Inn as Told by Joe Camp

Unlike most trainers, Frank Inn always relied on vocabulary. And comprehension of concept. Not mechanical, rote memory training. Not Pavlovian responses. He liked to say that he spoke to the animals the same way he talked to humans. While he trained them with rewards and hand signals, he also communicated with them in words. Clearly, his method of dog whispering worked. Animals willingly did what he asked them to do. For more about Frank Inn's methods, see Joe Camp's *The Benji Method: Teach Your Dog to Do What Benji Does in the Movies.*

The best training tip ever is another one I got from Frank Inn: teach your dog to sit and stay before you teach anything else. For a dog to sit and stay is the equivalent of being in a New York traffic jam, until you, the trainer, say it's okay to move. To sit and stay, even though you have turned your back and walked fifty feet away or into the next room. When you have accomplished that kind of comprehension, all the rest of your training will be very easy. (For more about Joe Camp, see his website, www.thesoulofahorse.com.)

Part 4

CAT STARS
AND THEIR TRAINERS

Charlie, one of the cats who played Mr. Jinx in *Little Fockers*

Cuddly cats, crazy cats, cat-astrophic cats. No matter how you describe them, cats are mystifying creatures who have fascinated humans for thousands of years. The Egyptians worshipped cats as gods. In movies, cats don't receive nearly that much adulation. Majestic wild cats portray raw power and incite fear. The domesticated cat, that little fur ball who pads quietly around the house and sidles next to a leg to take possession of her human, can't seem to land many starring roles. Filmmakers don't seem inclined to explore a cat's complex personality, except for maybe the film based on the musical *Cats*. And what an indignity — *humans* played those cat characters! Instead of adoring them, scriptwriters and directors usually put movie and TV house cats into stories for their comic or horror value.

While movie cats keep their secretive lives under wraps, the next section of this book reveals what motivates them to perform for filmed media. Although most people would wonder how anyone could train skittish and unpredictable cats, the following stories offer clues to the mysterious process. They show cats learning how to navigate around a scene and do tricks no one would ever expect.

Jim and Gina Brockett's story tells how they raised Cuff, a Siberian lynx, and gave him the task of charming supermodel Angie Everhart. Angie shared the spotlight with Cuff while draped in diamonds for a Cartier ad.

Besides Jim and Gina Brockett's Siberian lynx, you're going to have the pleasure of meeting Crackerjack. This red Persian cat became Emma Watson's

DID YOU KNOW...?

In 2013, Kwane Stewart, DVM, became chief veterinary officer and national director of the Film and Television Unit of American Humane Association (AHA). Dr. Stewart spearheads AHA's future for animal protection. He's charged with medical and scientific oversight of the No Animals Were Harmed certification program for animals in entertainment, and he reviews guidelines and standards to keep them in step with current animal needs.

companion on-screen as Crookshanks, Hermione's cat in the Harry Potter movies. Offscreen, Crackerjack formed a sweet friendship with Emma during petting sessions over their years working together on the films.

Kwane Stewart, DVM, chief veterinary officer and national director of AHA's Film and Television Unit, with his cat Sushi

You'll also learn training tips from premier cat trainer Dawn Barkan. Dawn adopted two rescued seal point Himalayans to play the role of Mr. Jinx in the Fockers series. They found a buddy in Robert De Niro, who played the Focker family patriarch and seemed to appreciate Peanut's and Charlie's cat consciousness. Dawn's cats even managed to flush the toilet and unlatch a baby's playpen.

Let the purrs begin.

Chapter 17

JULIE TOTTMAN

(LONG MARSTON, TRING, HERTFORDSHIRE, ENGLAND)

Julie Tottman training Crackerjack (Crookshanks)

Crackerjack as Crookshanks, Hermione's Cat in the Harry Potter Films
Right Cat for the Job

Julie Tottman

In the Harry Potter films, Hermione Granger, played by Emma Watson, has a red Persian cat named Crookshanks as her pet. In the book series, the cat is introduced in *Harry Potter and the Prisoner of Azkaban*. When Harry meets the flat-faced, ginger-colored, magical cat, he is amazed at Crookshanks's size and wonders if the cat might be a small tiger.

As the head animal trainer / coordinator for Birds and Animals UK, I was in charge of a team of seven people to train for the Harry Potter film series. We trained about 250 animals over eleven years, including the owls and hippos in the portraits of moving animals on the walls of Hogwarts School of Witchcraft and Wizardry.

For *Harry Potter and the Sorcerer's Stone*, I had to find a couple of red Persian cats to play Crookshanks. We always work with teams of animals that we can interchange for a role, because the animals need breaks from the hot lights on set. Also, one of the team might be better than another at a behavior, like running or sitting still, so it is necessary to have several cats to choose from for a scene.

I started looking for a cat to play Crookshanks by calling animal rescue centers. At an animal shelter, I found a body double who could stand in for Crookshanks to get the lighting right. But I still needed a cat who had exactly the red Persian coloring, facial features, and personality the producers needed. So I broadened my search and visited several breeders.

> **DID YOU KNOW...?**
>
> Computer-generated imagery (CGI) and special effects had a banner year in 2001, with the release of *Harry Potter and the Sorcerer's Stone* and *The Lord of the Rings: The Fellowship of the Ring*.

Crackerjack

As soon as I saw Crackerjack, I knew that he had not only the perfect look, but also the perfect nature. His fur was rich red, and he had huge amber eyes. He came bounding over to me like a dog. He was brave and full of mischief. I just knew he was the one.

Since cats can be nervous about moving from place to place, it is important to find a naturally bold cat for the job of animal actor. And the greedier the better. Crackerjack jumped onto my bag of chicken treats as soon as we met. This showed me that he would be eager to work for food as his reward.

Training Crackerjack

I learned how to match the right animals for the right roles during twenty years in my dream job as an animal trainer. From the time I worked at a pet beauty salon when I was fourteen years old, to volunteering to clean pet cages at animal-training companies, I had prepared for my life's work. I've always loved animals, and when I had my breakthrough, being hired for *101 Dalmatians* in 1996 and then as head puppy trainer for *102 Dalmatians*, I knew I had made it into the career I'd always wanted.

Now it was time to draw upon my experience and start training Crackerjack. I began by teaching basic obedience commands — sit, lie down, stay, and stay at a certain spot. Then we moved on to Crackerjack mastering how to hit certain marks, which could be a piece of wood, a stone, or a laser light beam on the ground.

We started training Crackerjack with a large piece of wood that we put his front feet on before giving him a treat. We then increased the distance so he was walking onto the wood without our tempting him. After he mastered distance, we gradually reduced the size of the wood piece. Once he knew that I would change and try different objects, he understood his mark could be anything I put out for him.

Crackerjack learned to run to buzzers and follow a buzzing sound. We train a cat with a buzzer by using a food reward. The cat needs to figure out that the buzzing indicates where a tasty treat will be. The cat then wants to find the buzzing sound and follow it. Recognizing and responding to a buzzer meant I could put one in Emma's pocket and Crackerjack would follow her anywhere.

The great thing about providing Crackerjack to play the part as Hermione's cat was the fact that Emma Watson was such a cat lover. Emma was besotted with Crackerjack from day one. She constantly cuddled him.

To achieve the mangy look Crookshanks was supposed to have, I saved the fur he shed. He went into makeup before each scene he was in.

Julie Tottman clicker-training Crackerjack

We had to make little fake mats to put in his fur so he would look matted. I clipped the mats in and out each time he performed.

Keeping Crackerjack Safe

I stayed with Crackerjack during the entire time he was on the set, to make sure he was always safe. A busy film set with people rushing around can be a strange place for a little cat. The cats need to learn to trust us. I am the eyes for cats and protect them from people's feet. We also shield them from hot lights and keep them away from sharp props and special effects.

When filming finished for the day, Crackerjack went back to Birds and Animals UK's facility at the studios, which has indoor and outdoor runs for the cats. Sofas, televisions, toys, and playmates keep the cat actors rested, amused, and socialized with each other.

On weekends and in between jobs, Crackerjack came home to live with me. He likes to be the leader at home. He knows he is special, so is forever demanding attention.

Given that Crackerjack remains in good health, he will work on other projects until he is around twelve years old. Then he will retire at my house. He had a small part in the movie *Hugo* and has done a few commercials since his Harry Potter days.

We are still waiting for the moment when Crackerjack is a main character. I'm anticipating that the bold red Persian cat who brought to life Hermione Granger's charming companion will play a starring role someday.

Tips for Training Cats
from Julie Tottman

My advice for training cats is to be kind, understanding, and patient. Be consistent and explain everything slowly to your cat. You cannot be in a hurry when you train or pet a cat.

To see a short video of me training Crackerjack to hit his marks, go to www.youtube.com/watch?v=woCHjh2WQn8.

Chapter 18

JIM AND GINA BROCKETT

(THOUSAND OAKS, CALIFORNIA)

and ANGIE EVERHART

Aspen, Jim and Gina's Canada lynx

Cuff as the Lynx with Angie Everhart and in *Evan Almighty*

Diamonds Are a Big Cat's Best Friend

Jim and Gina Brockett

Since 1978, when we started Bricketts Film Fauna, one of our most cherished animals was a Siberian lynx named Cuff (as in Cuff Lynx). Very intelligent and larger relatives of the bobcat, lynx are usually found in Europe, Asia, and the former USSR. A lynx like Cuff has yellowish fur and a pattern of spots covering his entire body.

Cuff did things house cats do but expressed her love bigger and better than the average feline. She rubbed against Gina, lowered her head, and purred with affection. Normally, wild cats work for a food reward. In the case of Cuff, her reward was Gina. We don't know many wild cats like Cuff. She would go from point A to point B just to be with Gina. We joked about the special relationship Cuff had with Gina when Jim said, "I want to be Gina's lynx."

We raised Cuff in our house from the time she was six weeks old. She shared her home with our bobcat, Ninja, and our Siamese cat, Tuyun. They all played together. We enjoyed taking Cuff and Willow, a Canada lynx, on leashes for long walks every day.

Angie Everhart and Cuff

When Cuff did a photo session with supermodel Angie Everhart, the model wore five million dollars' worth of Cartier diamonds. The shoot was in Benedict Canyon, a suburb of Los Angeles. To introduce Cuff to Angie, we all rode to the location with Cuff loose in our van. Angie and Cuff became comfortable with each other during the drive. Gina could tell by watching Angie and Cuff that everyone was safe. On set, we kept Cuff surrounded by people with whom she was familiar.

A guard came with the Cartier diamonds, along with a small group

Gina Brockett and Cuff

of about a dozen people. Cuff wasn't paying attention to anyone, though. She had spotted a deer randomly walking down a nearby path. She focused on, and turned direction to lock onto, the deer and wouldn't look at anything else.

In the wild, a cat can't stalk ten animals at once. As a survival mechanism, he has to pick one and not break his concentration while hunting it. Wild cats sometimes fixate on one person out of a hundred extras on a film set, and the cat won't look at the trainers, only at that person. On one shoot, we had to ask for an extra to be sent home because the cat was obsessing on that person.

We were fortunate the day of the Cartier shoot. Because she was focusing on the deer walking past the set, Cuff was not distracted by the photographer, his assistant, or anything else. The Cartier diamond project was a great success. And Angie Everhart was wonderful with our affectionate lynx.

A Married Couple's Shared Career

After we met and married, we dedicated ourselves to rescuing animals like Cuff and working in the film industry. Animal control and the California Department of Fish and Wildlife regularly bring rescues to

Film Fauna. Ours is one of the few facilities in California that is legally permitted to care for exotic animals. Most of our thirty alligators are rescues. They come to us because a lot of people from other states, where it is not illegal to have alligators as pets, move to California. Here, if they can't get a legal state permit, they must relinquish the alligators. Also, neighbors, post office mail deliverers, meter readers, and others who visit people's houses contact authorities or call zoos when they spot an alligator. If we can't take the rescued alligators into our facility, they have to be euthanized. This is why we have so many of them. In addition, we have rescued snakes, tortoises, bobcats, birds, and a capybara — a one-hundred-pound guinea pig, the largest rodent in the world — who came to us from Agoura Animal Shelter.

Our employees are graduates of Moorpark College Exotic Animal Training and Management Program. At the college, they learn the skills of working with exotic animals and then go on to work in businesses such as ours, zoos, or other animal-related industries.

Jim, who has a bachelor's degree in zoology, specializes in reptiles. Reptiles don't develop attachments the way mammals do. People might believe that their pet boa constrictor loves them, but reptiles are not emotional. They get used to being handled by certain people. Alligators and crocodiles recognize people but are not affectionate toward them.

Our company provides a rattlesnake safety service to help protect cast and crew when they are filming in remote locations. We also work with birds, butterflies, insects, spiders, frogs, and other species on our five-acre ranch in the Santa Monica Mountains, where we make our home.

Gina's Protection

Gina specializes in small wild cats like Cuff. She is their caretaker and protector. One time, the director of an automobile commercial wanted our bobcat to run into the desert. The camera on a helicopter would pan over the moving car.

Gina explained that he couldn't have a cat running in the desert from one point to nowhere. There needed to be a destination. Someone had to catch the cat.

The director didn't believe the hovering helicopter would bother the cat. He seemed to think the animal had no awareness, as if our bobcat was one of the props, a widget that could be dealt with like an inanimate object. He hadn't entertained the idea that there might be other things to consider when working with a living being.

On another shoot, Cuff was to do a European car ad in the desert. Jim told the director that they'd need to start the shoot by 7:00 AM and be finished by 10:00 AM, because Cuff couldn't work after it became too hot. The director showed up at 9:00 AM with his crew in air-conditioned motor homes. By the time he decided he wanted Cuff to sit in the middle of the road, it was nearing 11:00 in the morning. Cuff sat a couple of times and then got up and walked off.

The director asked, "Why won't the cat sit in the road?"

Gina answered, "Pull *your* pants down and see how long *you* could sit on hot pavement. The cat's not going to sit on the hot road." We offered to put a furniture pad down on the *side*, not the middle of the paved road, where Cuff could sit comfortably.

This director's lack of knowledge about animals is the kind of issue we contend with occasionally. We must draw our parameters for how the animal actors will work. Our motto is "Don't do stupid things, and bad things won't happen."

Cuff and *Evan Almighty*

Cuff worked in the film *Evan Almighty*. In the movie, God (Morgan Freeman) contacted Buffalo, New York, congressman Evan Baxter (Steve Carell) and told him to build an ark and prepare for a great flood. Soon, pairs of animals started showing up in his yard. *Evan Almighty* was the most expensive comedy ever made, and the producers spent a great deal of money on the animals.

Cuff was one of the animals to board Evan's ark. Her work was mostly done in front of a blue screen, and she didn't interact much with other actors. With blue screen, the animal is photographed against a solid blue background. When the film is developed, the blue color is excluded, leaving only the photographed animal. That image can then be added to any background.

Film Fauna Animals on TV

When experts from National Geographic or Animal Planet bring animals on television shows such as *The Tonight Show with Jay Leno* or *Late Night with Conan O'Brien*, the experts don't travel across the country with animals. Instead, they ask Film Fauna to supply animals that they will talk about on the shows.

Our latest addition to Film Fauna is our wonderful young bobcat Ruby Rose. She made her debut at six months old on *Late Night with Conan O'Brien* with National Geographic presenter Casey Anderson. Most recently, she was on the TV show *Bones*, acting as a wild bobcat!

Ruby Rose and Aspen, our Canada lynx, were raised together. They love to race around our patio and play.

Film Fauna's bobcat Ruby Rose with Casey Anderson on *Late Night with Conan O'Brien*

Keeping Animals and People Safe

Anyone who works with wild animals should never get complacent. People with big cats or chimps think the animal has been their friend for a long time, but this doesn't mean a wild animal won't suddenly come unglued. Tragic accidents happen to a lot of people who forget that the animals they have brought into their homes are dangerous, powerful, and very smart. After ten years of a chimp being their best friend, all of a sudden, he is not. Little wild cats are like two-year-olds with loaded guns. They might never pull the trigger, but they still don't make good pets.

On every film shoot with animals, we set things up with safety always in mind. We keep production people from upsetting the animals. We won't put an animal into a situation unless we are sure they can handle it.

There are a lot of misconceptions about animal actors and their trainers. If a stunt person has an accident, it's just considered bad luck. If an animal has an accident on a film set, some people assume it's because of how the animal was trained. You can't successfully train by abuse. If you did that, the animal would cower. An abusive relationship is very easy to spot, and the animal would come across as fearful on film.

We have always had a good relationship with American Humane Association (AHA). If a situation comes up that we don't want to deal with, we tell AHA safety representatives that we won't do what is requested. That takes us out of the equation. Most of AHA's regulations and guidelines are reasonable. They have a tough job, and they do it well.

Cuff and
Gina Brockett (holding
Willow on her lap)

We got a call from the *Wall Street Journal* when they were writing an article about AHA's new guidelines for animal safety. The reporter asked Gina to comment on the fact that no animal in a film, not even an ant or a fly, is allowed to be killed. Gina explained that she agreed with the policy, saying, "Where do you draw the line? If you kill an ant, then is it okay to kill a goldfish, a mouse, or a cat? No, we don't kill anything for film."

Cuff, a Family Member

Cuff lived with us on the ranch for twelve years. Unfortunately, in 2007, we lost our beautiful Siberian lynx. Everyone we consulted thought that Cuff had a treatable thyroid condition. We spent thousands of dollars on veterinarian care before she was finally diagnosed with brain cancer.

The hardest part of living with animals you love is that you are probably going to outlive them. We've lost a member of our family.

Tips for Training Cats
from Gina Brockett

The main thing with training cats is to start very young. If the cats are already on their own and independent, it's harder to bond with them. We always begin our training with weaned cats when they are about six weeks old.

Because our cats travel to locations in kennels, we train them at an early age to go to a crate for food. This gets them comfortable with riding. We also train them to go to a buzzer.

Although we continue training cats with food, Cuff and other small cats work more from trust of, and affection for, their trainer than for food. Big cats work strictly for food.

Little cats have a shorter fuse. They are more tightly wound animals. They lose their temper more quickly than a big cat. You have to work around bad behavior and can't reprimand little cats, because they take it personally and get in a bad mood fast. Little cats go into fight mode immediately. It's just the way they are wired.

Big cats are more even tempered. You can reprimand cats such as lions, tigers, and leopards for bad behavior, and they'll learn from it.

Bonus: Tips for Handling Reptiles
from Jim Brockett

Reptiles make great pets. They are low maintenance. Plan to treat them like tropical fish in that you can't expect to bond with them. They won't be affectionate like a mammal or bird.

Get a cage that will be big enough for a grown reptile so you don't have to buy a series of cages. Some people buy a baby python without asking how big the snake gets. They are shocked when the python grows large enough to eat a dog.

If you buy a reptile (or any pet) on impulse, it usually turns out badly. Do your homework before buying a reptile. Learn as much as you can about their care requirements. Reptiles are tropical and have to be kept at a certain temperature. They need the right food. Most reptiles need ultraviolet lights. They don't do well outdoors.

Cuff and Cartier

Angie Everhart

First of all, if there is an animal lover, it is I. When I was asked to do the Cartier diamond ad, I jumped at the chance to be photographed with a full-grown lynx!

However, when I got to the shoot, it was a bit tricky. We were in the woods, and Cuff was much bigger than I had anticipated. One never knows what a wild animal will do, so we were cautious not to move around like crazy or scare the cat.

The photo shoot went relatively fast, and the trainers were right there, hands on, to assure the animal that everything was okay.

I wanted to take Cuff home with me, but I am sure my dogs would not have appreciated it.

What is better than working with an amazing animal while covered in diamonds?!

Angie Everhart

Chapter 19

DAWN BARKAN

(NEWTON, NEW JERSEY)

Peanut and Robert De Niro

Peanut and Charlie as Mr. Jinx
in *Meet the Fockers* and *Little Fockers*
Cool Cats

Dawn Barkan

In 1999, I got an assignment to train cats for *Meet the Parents*. That movie started the popular series about the Byrnes and Fockers, two larger-than-life families brought together through the marriage of a son and daughter. In the film, starring Robert De Niro, Ben Stiller, Blythe Danner, Teri Polo, and Owen Wilson, the Byrnes family has a personality-plus cat named Mr. Jinx. The first cats I trained to play the role of Mr. Jinx were Misha, Stella, and Chewy. They came from Larry Madrid, a coworker who had trained them.

All the cats excelled at playing Mr. Jinx in the first Fockers movie, but Misha turned out to be phenomenal. Misha was willing and able to do everything I asked of him. He performed 90 percent of everything Mr. Jinx's character was supposed to do. Even though seal point Himalayans are not the most agile and tend to be lap kitties, Misha turned out to be quite athletic. He even had a scene in which he had to climb a two-story trellis covered in ivy. This was quite a feat, since he was an indoor cat and not used to scaling fences and trees. In my opinion, Misha was the star of the movie. Because of his intelligence, physical prowess, and work ethic, I fell in love with Himalayans and think they are great cats.

Animals and Other Family Members

I love animals and have had them in my life since childhood. For me, training animal actors is more of a privilege than anything else. I do animal training for Birds and Animals Unlimited.

When our family was about to welcome our first child, I got the job of training cats for *Meet the Fockers*, the second movie in the series. At that time, my husband, Cort Hessler, and I lived with eight dogs and five cats in our home.

After we brought our daughter Olivia home from the hospital, people advised us to separate her from our pets. But that advice was contrary to everything I knew as a trainer. I thought that keeping my daughter from the animals would cause her to become something of interest and make her stand out. I believed that the best way to have family harmony would be to let my daughter become a natural part of "the pack," as if her arrival was no big deal. I didn't change the animals' schedules, restrict them, or disrupt their lives. They accepted Olivia because the baby hadn't caused any interruption in their routines. Now I take my daughter to movie sets, where she helps me by buzzing buzzers and opening crates. For a working mom with a career that I love, it has been a pleasure to watch Olivia fit into it so well.

Training Cat Actors

I am all about building relationships between people and animals. Before you can ask an animal to do anything for you, it is important to establish trust. That way, no matter what happens on a movie set, the animal knows that I am a place of safety. So I spend time with the animals I train by bringing them home to live with my family and share my space. They lie in bed with me. We watch television together. I let them relax into the environment and get to know me. I pick up the cats; bathe, brush, and groom them; and sit quietly with them until they feel completely comfortable. Sometimes, I just sit in a room with the cats and don't say a word. If they want to approach me, they can; if they don't, that's fine, too. I invite cats who have been entrusted to my care for a movie to become part of my family.

It's only after they are comfortable that I start the training process. By then, the cats know I won't ask for anything hurtful or scary or something that would be impossible for them to handle. They have learned that our relationship isn't only about work. We will always have downtime and playtime.

Some animals enjoy working more than others. Some personalities are very easygoing, and a trainer can get along with them right away. Other personalities are a little tougher, and the animal and trainer might not click immediately. The trainer has to adjust to the individual animal.

Cats are driven by their ears. When they hear a loud or strange sound, they run away. As part of their training, I expose them to the sounds they'll experience on a set before we ever have our first day at work. Prior to their first jobs, after they are familiar with their new home, I take the cats for rides with me, since we will travel by car to work on a set. I positively condition them by going through the process of getting ready for their work often enough that when it is time to do the real thing, they are prepared and not afraid. As I put the cats in their crates and carry them out the door, they know something fun and interesting is about to happen.

Peanut

Because Misha was getting older and had some health issues, he needed to retire to a good home where he would live out his life as someone's beloved pet. So I searched on the animal adoption website Petfinder.com for the next seal point Himalayan to play Jinx. I found Peanut living in an animal shelter in Virginia. The woman who had relinquished her was pregnant and didn't want a cat in the house with her baby. I drove to Virginia and adopted Peanut.

Peanut did 90 percent of the scenes in *Meet the Fockers*; an older Himalayan named Diamond served as her double. Peanut turned out to be not only a sweet soul but also a fantastic animal actor. The scene in the movie in which Mr. Jinx perches on the seat and flushes the toilet became a comedy classic.

If an animal actor is at point A in a scene and the trainer releases him to go to point B, that is a straightforward task. But if the animal must perform several actions in sequence, this is known as a pattern. Peanut turned out to be a pro at doing patterns. For one scene, she had to walk into a room, circle the baby's exercise pen, jump up, pull herself up on her back legs, reach with her front legs for a latch, unlatch it, and then run away.

Peanut flushing a toilet
in *Meet the Fockers*

There's not much I'd be afraid to ask Peanut to do for a role, because based on what I've seen her accomplish, I think she could figure it out. It's ironic that the pregnant woman, who didn't want Peanut around her new baby, gave up a cat who could unlatch a toddler's exercise pen. Sometimes, I wonder if the woman has any idea what a great cat she missed out on.

Charlie

I always train teams of cats for a role so no one cat has to do too much. Because Diamond would have to retire due to old age, I needed another cat to work with Peanut on *Little Fockers*, the next movie in the series. I returned to Petfinder.com and found Charlie, also a seal point Himalayan, at the Leeds and Grenville branch of the Ontario Society for the Prevention of Cruelty to Animals in Canada. Charlie had been roaming the streets of the city, perfectly groomed. The shelter posted his picture and put out bulletins, but nobody claimed him.

I explained to the animal-shelter staff what I do and that I'd be training Charlie to be a movie animal. The shelter agreed to meet me midway in Syracuse, New York, so I could adopt Charlie. Another trainer and I drove up to Syracuse to bring Charlie home. On the first day, he took over our house and told everyone, even the dogs, "I live here now. Deal with it."

To this day, Charlie is a phenomenal personality in our home. He has no idea he's a cat and thinks he's a dog. He gets up on my bed with my other cats and dogs, makes them move over, and demands room for himself. He's a real prima donna.

While other cats might be timid and get startled if they hear grips dropping things or gaffers pulling cords on a movie set, Charlie's first instinct isn't to escape. He's in charge, no matter what might be happening. Because he thinks he is top cat and everyone must treat him that way, he blends into the activities on set without caring what is going on around him. Charlie just comes in and does his job. The atmosphere can be more relaxed with a cat as unflappable as Charlie.

Charlie came through with grace and ease on his first assignment. He and Peanut each played about half the role of Mr. Jinx in *Little Fockers*. Since then, Charlie has been in the movie *Proud Iza* and a sketch on Comedy Central in the role opposite a cat whisperer who tries unsuccessfully to train him. Charlie's first rejection came when director Nora Ephron wouldn't hire him to play Amy Adams's cat in *Julie & Julia*. Nora thought Charlie looked like too much of a fancy cat to be a pet for the character Julie Powell, who lived in a cramped New York apartment.

Cats on a Movie Set

I don't think animals actually act for a movie role. They are responding to what the trainer asks them to do. There are some animals who understand being on set, though. They are completely different during the shooting process than when we are preparing for a scene. They seem to realize that the camera is on, and their energy level gets higher. Perhaps they are reading the energy of people around them and realize they are at work now. Many animal actors understand the word *action*. After they hear it several times, they know it means that it is time to go.

When a cat is called to be in a scene, he might not feel energetic. He's a cat, after all. He will only move when he feels like it. So I use cues, like buzzers or clickers, to raise his excitement level. Calling his name in a high voice can get the cat interested and ready. I might look a little odd, standing in front of a crate and saying, "Kitty, kitty, kitty," in a high voice, then running backward, but it amps up the cat. He springs out of his crate with high energy.

When animal actors get older or if they have health problems, it is time for them to become family pets. If the cats are no longer able to work or acting doesn't seem to be fun for them anymore, they retire. Our movie animals spend the rest of their days being happy cats. Charlie and Peanut are still, and will always be, part of my family. Peanut retired at the ripe old cat age of fifteen.

Tips for Training Cats from Dawn Barkan

People are often surprised that a cat can be trained. But I find that some of them enjoy having a task to do. It breaks up the monotony of their day. Experiencing something different motivates them.

Always take the time to build confidence when attempting to train cats. The more you rush or push them, the more anxious and less trusting they become.

Meet cats at their level, and they will respond to you much better than if you get into a power struggle with them.

Cats' driving force is food, and they will work for it as a reward. So make training fun, use food as an incentive, and you may find that your cat looks forward to learning new tricks and behaviors.

Afterword

HOW YOU CAN HELP
TOMORROW'S ANIMAL STARS

Y ou have had the opportunity to look at movies, television, and commercials through the eyes of animal stars, and you may be wondering how you can contribute to keeping them safe and healthy. Even though you can't personally be on a set to monitor the action, you can support the wonderful people whose sole purpose for being there is to protect animals.

The following is a step-by-step process for making yourself part of the solution and encouraging filmmakers to put animal care at the top of their priority list.

First, ask friends, family, and social networks to join you in encouraging filmmakers to continue hiring professional trainers and animal actors and working in close cooperation with American Humane Association (AHA). Letters, blogs, emails, and articles are powerful tools for letting filmmakers know that you have a choice about how to spend your time and entertainment dollars. Let everyone know that when animal actors are being treated with care and respect, it influences your decisions about which movies to see and programs to watch. Let filmmakers know when you enjoy seeing an animal in entertainment, and that you enjoy seeing the power of the human-animal bond on-screen.

Second, go to the movie database at www.humanehollywood.org/index .php/movie-reviews on the AHA website. In 1998, the website began to provide filmgoers with movie reviews that describe how animal action was achieved. The website includes a ratings system, a mechanism for people to ask questions and raise concerns, and information for producers on how and why to register their films and request the assistance of AHA safety representatives.

You can look up a movie or television program and find out how AHA rated it. AHA movie and television show reviews are unlike any others you have ever read. Instead of focusing on the writing, acting, and directing skills, AHA reviews explain how the animal action was done, why AHA considered it safe or not, and what level of protection the animals received. Again, encourage producers and directors to have AHA safety representatives on set and to cooperate with them in every way for the safety of animals.

> Not sure how to contact producers and directors? Go to www.imdb .com. This is an international database that lists movies, casts, and crew. When you find the name of a producer, actor, or director, click on it for more information. Do an internet search for the producer's company. Make an extra effort to correctly spell names, and send your encouraging letters to working email addresses or use production company website contact forms.

Third, consider becoming a member of American Humane Association. The AHA Film and Television Unit works early in the process to act as a credible witness to the humane treatment of animal actors where and when they are allowed to do so.

Jon Turteltaub, director of the first and second *National Treasure* movies, summed up the opinion he shares with many of his Hollywood colleagues when he said, "Nothing should be harmed to make a movie. It's a movie. Nothing should be hurt. Nothing should be killed. You don't want to go to bed ever with that on you. So give yourself that break. Have American Humane Association [on your sets]."

The Past, Present, and Future

In 1980, AHA issued *Guidelines for the Safe Use of Animals Working in Filmed Entertainment*, its first formalized guidelines for using "sentient beasts" in addition to humans as actors. By 2009, the guidelines had expanded to a 128-page book covering every aspect of production, including preplanning, on-set production, and postproduction of filmed media that involve animal (or insect) action. As new science and proven practices that affect animal health and behavior emerge, the safety guidelines and standards evolve and are updated.

Animals don't have the ability to say in words when they are sick or something hurts. They can't voice opinions or fears that an action or behavior a director wants from them may cause injury. AHA, with recommendations from its science advisory board and teams of respected animal experts, defines what is safe or potentially harmful on the sets of television, film, and commercial filming. Along with professional trainers and caring actors and directors, they combine affection for animals with professionalism, experience, independence, and education. In the process, AHA representatives speak for the animals, who, no matter how well they act on- and offscreen, haven't yet learned to speak in a language that directors understand.

The future is looking brighter for animals and professional trainers, with AHA making strides toward a more comprehensive approach to animal actor welfare. Kwane Stewart, DVM, chief veterinary officer and national director of the Film and Television Unit, is in charge of upgrading animal actor safety guidelines. He says, "With an objective, third-party point of view, we can be involved from the beginning of an animal actor's life to the animal's retirement. We can work on safeguards for how animal actors are raised and trained. It's important to us to be able to give the public some reassurance about the ways animals are being cared for on and off set."

Expanding efforts to keep animal actors safe and healthy includes having veterinarians, like Dr. Stewart, on sets and visiting facilities where animal actors live when they are not working. AHA veterinarians and veterinary technicians can help assess which animals might need medical attention. AHA, using current scientific and medical expertise, can define what is potentially harmful to animal actors and take care of them in real time.

We sincerely hope that you enjoyed this book's behind-the-scenes peek at the lives and personalities of animal stars. We also hope you will take action to support AHA, as well as the filmmakers and trainers who have dedicated themselves to keeping animals safe. The animal actors can only thank you with their magnificent performances. But we thank you from the bottom of our hearts for joining us in ensuring the safety and care of animals in filmed media.

Appendix

DISCUSSION QUESTIONS
FOR BOOK CLUBS

The following questions can serve as guides for book clubs and study groups when they discuss the themes of *Animal Stars*.

What is the most interesting movie, television program, or commercial with animal action you have ever seen? Why?

What animal actor stories in this book surprised you the most? Which stories did you find the most heartwarming?

Did you know that many animal stars were found in local shelters or through breed-specific animal rescue groups before being adopted and trained for filmed media work?

What traits do you think professional animal trainers look for in a shelter dog or cat as a potential animal actor?

What training tips from the professional animal trainers in this book do you think you will apply to your own pets or the animals in your care?

Why isn't it a good idea for amateurs, or people with no professional education or experience in keeping animal actors safe, to bring their pets or other animals to work on a set?

Mark Harden's Chico
in the park

What do you think should happen for animal actors after their careers
working in filmed media are finished?

Have you been inspired by this book to take action? What will you
do to express appreciation to filmmakers and movie and television producers who register their productions with American
Humane Association (AHA) and ask AHA certified animal
safety representatives to monitor their projects?

Would you recommend this book to others? Why? Who would
appreciate or benefit from receiving your gift of *Animal Stars*?

ACKNOWLEDGMENTS

This book has supporters who have helped us bring it to life and invite readers to its pages. Robin Ganzert would especially like to thank Marty Becker, DVM, for his contributions. In addition to the incredibly generous Steven Spielberg, thanks to Julia Roberts, Ewan McGregor, Hailee Steinfeld, and Angie Everhart for contributing stories for this book even in the midst of their immensely busy lives. Thanks to Richard Gere for his photo on the book cover.

The entertainment community has been unwavering in its commitment to keeping animals safe in filmed media. Special thanks go to the American Federation of Television and Radio Artists (AFTRA) Industry Cooperative Fund; the Screen Actors Guild–Producers Industry Advancement and Cooperative Fund; Ilyanne Morden Kichaven, executive director, Los Angeles local, Screen Actors Guild–American Federation of Television and Radio Artists (SAG-AFTRA); Ken Howard, copresident, SAG-AFTRA; and Roberta Reardon, copresident, SAG-AFTRA.

The authors are grateful to the American Humane Association (AHA) board of directors for its advice and support, as well as to the Humane Hollywood Scientific Advisory Committee; AHA's certified animal safety representatives, who work diligently for the protection of animals in film and entertainment; Kwane Stewart, DVM, chief veterinary officer and national director of AHA's Film and Television Unit; and Karen Rosa, senior adviser for AHA's Film and Television Unit.

The professional animal trainers in this book participated in this project with their contributions of time, effort, generosity, and unceasing commitment to the animals in their care. We feel an immense appreciation for them and their work.

To Todd Krim of The Krim Group, Larry McAllister of Paramount Pictures, Mary Hulett of DreamWorks, and Melanie Murray of ID-PR, thank you for opening doors to many of the world's most well-known and respected stars.

We would like to thank the staff at New World Library, including president Marc Allen; vice president and marketing director Munro Magruder; our amazing executive editor, Georgia Hughes; energetic and efficient senior publicist Monique Muhlenkamp; managing editor Kristen Cashman; type designer Tona Pearce Myers; cover designer Tracy Cunningham; copyeditor Mark Colucci; proofreader Karen Stough; assistant editor Jonathan Wichmann; and all the rest of the New World Library staff.

We extend our heartfelt gratitude to Stephanie Kip Rostan of Levine Greenberg Literary Agency Inc., our patient and wise literary agent, who believed in this book from its inception.

Allen and Linda Anderson want to especially thank their mothers, Bobbie Anderson and Gertrude Jackson; their daughter and son, Susan Anderson and Mun Anderson; and their animal companions over the years, who were among their greatest healers and teachers.

Robin Ganzert especially thanks the Ganzert family, who provides her with daily inspiration, and Rob and Linda Roy, who taught her what it is to be humane.

ENDNOTES

Part 1

Page 12 *"Animals need an advocate"*: "Award Winning Director Quentin Tarantino Is a Huge Fan of American Humane Association," YouTube video, 1:45, posted by "americanhumane," January 22, 2013, www.youtube.com/watch?v=mVrK 5T_k4lA.

Page 22 *"The thing that I kept emphasizing"*: "Celebrities Support American Humane Association's No Animals Were Harmed Certification Program," YouTube video, 4:12, posted by "americanhumane," January 17, 2013, www.youtube.com /watch?v=MAD7Q-nn5K8.

Page 37 *"American Humane Association has fought"*: Ibid.

Part 2

Page 45 *"I think the animals are taken for granted"*: "Celebrities Support American Humane Association's No Animals Were Harmed Certification Program," YouTube video, 4:12, posted by "americanhumane," January 17, 2013, www.you tube.com/watch?v=MAD7Q-nn5K8.

Page 52 *"There are always shortcuts"*: Ibid.

Page 72 *"The animals were not put in any danger"*: Ibid.

Page 84 *"We followed the guidelines"*: Ibid.

Page 103 *"I just wanted everyone to know"*: Ibid.

Page 130 *"I have been in productions with animals"*: "AFTRA, American Humane

Association: Partners in Protecting Animals on Set," *AFTRA Magazine*, Summer 2010, 23.

Part 3

Page 153 *"Theaters posted death notices"*: Susan Orlean, *Rin Tin Tin: The Life and the Legend* (New York: Simon & Schuster, 2011), 112.

Page 153 *from sequenced photographs in 1882*: Ibid., 315.

Page 175 *"It was so good to have American Humane"*: "Celebrities Support American Humane Association's No Animals Were Harmed Certification Program," YouTube video, 4:12, posted by "americanhumane," January 17, 2013, www.you tube.com/watch?v=MAD7Q-nn5K8.

Page 214 *Together, Frank Inn, Higgins, and Joe Camp*: Factual information about Frank Inn, Higgins, and Benji was found in the following publications and verified in October 2013 by Joe Camp, producer of the Benji movies (www.benji.com): Joe Camp's unpublished letter to Frank Inn from Mulberry Square Productions, September 28, 1973; Sheila Jackson, "Benji and Trainer Frank Inn: The Golden Years," *Greater Burbank Visitors Guide*, First Quarter 1984, 9–10; Isabelle Caron, "At $7.43 an Hour, It's a Dog's Life," *TV Times*, November 4, 1970, 41–43; "A Tribute to Frank Inn" (program notes, American Humane Association presentation, Disneyland Hotel, Anaheim, California, October 4, 1998); Jon Thurber, "Frank Inn, 86; Trained Benji the Dog," *Los Angeles Times*, July 29, 2002; Douglas Martin, "Frank Inn, Who Trained Lassie and Benji, Is Dead at 86," *New York Times*, August 4, 2002, www.nytimes.com/2002/08/04/nyregion/frank -inn-who-trained-lassie-and-benji-is-dead-at-86.html; Angielyn Hamilton-Lowe, "The Trainer Who Created Four-Legged Stars," NPR, June 28, 2012, www.npr.org /2012/07/27/155949615/the-trainer-who-created-four-legged-stars; "Benji Facts," accessed October 18, 2013, www.benji.com/BenjiFacts05.htm; "Frank Inn," *Wikipedia*, last modified October 28, 2013, http://en.wikipedia.org/wiki /Frank_Inn.

Page 221 *see* Joe Camp's The Phenomenon of Benji: Frank Inn, *Joe Camp's The Phenomenon of Benji* (New York: Bantam Books, 1977).

Page 223 *see Joe Camp's* The Benji Method: Joe Camp, *The Benji Method: Teach Your Dog to Do What Benji Does in the Movies*, 2nd ed. (14 Hands Press, 2011).

Afterword

Page 254 *"Nothing should be harmed"*: "Celebrities Support American Humane Association's No Animals Were Harmed Certification Program," YouTube video, 4:12, posted by "americanhumane," January 17, 2013, www.youtube.com /watch?v=MAD7Q-nn5K8.

CONTRIBUTING AUTHORS

Dawn Barkan ("Peanut and Charlie as Mr. Jinx in *Meet the Fockers* and *Little Fockers*: Cool Cats") has been a professional animal trainer for Birds and Animals Unlimited since 1989 and is now doing freelance projects for the company. Her cat-training methods have been featured in an Associated Press article, on PEOPLEPets.com, and on ABC News. Most of the animal actors she trains and cares for in her home are rescued from animal shelters.

Animal actors trained by Dawn have appeared in films and television shows, including a sketch for *Saturday Night Live*. Dawn has been animal coordinator, trainer, wrangler, handler, or head animal trainer for movies and television shows such as *Meet the Parents*; *Meet the Fockers*; *Little Fockers*; *Men in Black II*; *Garfield*; *Blue Bloods* (two episodes); *Old Dogs*; and *Inside Llewyn Davis*, among others. For a list of Dawn's credits, see www.imdb.com/name/nm0054772/.

Marty Becker, DVM (Foreword), known as "America's Veterinarian," is a nationally syndicated columnist, chief veterinary correspondent for and founding member of Core Team Oz for *The Dr. Oz Show*, adjunct professor at three colleges of veterinary medicine, board member of American Humane Association, and author of twenty-two books, including three *New York Times* bestsellers, that have sold more than 7 million copies.

Steve Berens ("Abbey as Sam in *I Am Legend*: Will Smith's Canine Costar") is president of Steve Berens' Animals of Distinction, Inc., a small company with over thirty years' experience that specializes in providing trained dogs and cats for all kinds of productions but also works with farm animals and exotics. He has worked in various parts of the United States as well as Africa, Australia, Brazil, Canada, the Czech Republic, Denmark, Italy, Mexico, and Turkey. For more about Animals of Distinction, see www.berensanimals.com.

Steve has been an animal wrangler, animal trainer, animal coordinator, head trainer, or dog trainer for *I Am Legend*; *Paranormal Activity 2, 3,* and *4*; *Twilight*; *The 25th Hour*; *Little Nicky*; *The Mask*; *Son of the Mask*; *Anger Management*; *The Truth about Cats & Dogs*; *The Boy Who Could Fly*; *Cougar Town*; twenty episodes of *Red Shoe Diaries*; and other productions. For a list of Steve's credits, see www.imdb.me/steveberens and www.berens animals.com/Credits.html.

Jim and Gina Brockett ("Cuff as the Lynx with Angie Everhart and in *Evan Almighty*: Diamonds Are a Big Cat's Best Friend") rescue animals and work in the film business. They are members of the International Animal Welfare Association, a nonprofit organization dedicated to preserving the rights of responsible, legal, permitted animal owners. Jim is a herpetological consultant for Natural Balance Pet Food Company, where he developed a nutritional diet for snakes and lizards.

Jim and Gina started Film Fauna in 1978. Film Fauna provides animals for film, television, print ads, and other occasions, including the cats and dogs for Petco flyers. Jim and Gina have been animal wranglers or trainers for the Animal Planet and Discovery channels, as well as the television shows *True Blood*; *Big Love*; *The Bold and the Beautiful*; *Untamed & Uncut*; *Bones*; *The Mentalist*; and *Buffy the Vampire Slayer*.

The Brocketts' company has provided guest animals for experts to show on *Late Night with Conan O'Brien*; *The Tonight Show with Jay Leno*; *Live with Regis and Kelly*; *Ellen*; and *Larry King Live*. They have wrangled, trained, or supplied animals for films including *Dorfman in Love*; *The Shaggy Dog*; *National Lampoon's Gold Diggers*; *My Sister's Keeper*; *Maverick*; *Happy Gilmore*; *The Player*; and *Mortal Kombat*. For a list of their credits, see www.imdb.com/name/nm0110670/. You can view Film Fauna's animals and insects for movies, television, and ads at www.facebook.com /pages/Brocketts-Film-Fauna/145583604594.

Sue Chipperton ("Gidget as the Taco Bell Dog: A Personality-Plus Chihuahua") is a trainer for Studio Animal Services and has worked for the company for close to twenty years. She has been an animal trainer, head or lead animal trainer, animal wrangler, animal coordinator, dog trainer, head dog trainer, or lead duck trainer for the feature films *Godzilla* (2014); *Shark Night 3D*; *The Ugly Truth*; *Gran Torino*; *Hancock*; *Déjà Vu*; *Memoirs of a Geisha*; *Duck*; *Lemony Snicket's A Series of Unfortunate Events*; *Win a Date with Tad Hamilton!*; *Sideways*; *Legally Blonde* and *Legally Blonde 2: Red, White & Blonde*; *Moonlight Mile*; *Six Days Seven Nights*; *The Fan*; *Crimson Tide*; *Se7en*; and others. She has worked on commercials for Purina; Friskies; Aflac; Pedigree; Travelers; Target; Kibbles 'n Bits; Capital One; Taco Bell; Meow Mix; Petco; PetSmart; Budweiser; California Cheese; and other companies. For more of Sue's credits, see www.imdb .com/name/nm0158077/.

Sue is coauthor of *A Famous Dog's Life*, the story of Gidget, the adorable Taco Bell dog, with a foreword by Reese Witherspoon, a TODAY Book Club selection. Sue and Gidget have been featured in articles and stories for national newspapers, magazines, major network news shows, wire services, websites, video clips, and blogs. You can see Gidget in a Taco Bell commercial at www.youtube.com/watch?v=BooEwoIMLXI and hear Sue talking about Gidget at www.petliferadio.com/sue_chipperton.html.

Sue was recently asked by www.thecityfarm.com to design collars and leashes for her own pet collection.

Sarah Clifford ("Training Uggie for *The Artist*: A Team Approach") is the owner of Animal Savvy and a highly respected set animal trainer, animal coordinator, and wrangler of animals for movies, television, commercials, and print shoots.

Sarah was a head animal trainer for the Academy Award–winning movie *The Artist*, where she worked alongside Omar von Muller and his Jack Russell terrier Uggie. Her credits include being animal coordinator, head animal trainer, or set production assistant for *A Haunted House* and *A Haunted House 2*; *Camp X-Ray*; *Hitchcock*; *Seeking a Friend for the End of the World*; *Pirates of the Caribbean: The Curse of the Black Pearl*; *The Matrix Reloaded*; and many other movies. For more about Sarah, see www.animalsavvy .net and www.imdb.com/name/nm0166683/.

Mathilde de Cagny ("Cosmo as Arthur in *Beginners*: The Dog Who Connected a Father and Son" and "Blackie, Enzo, and Borsalino as Maximilian in *Hugo*: Worthy of a Golden Collar") has worked for Birds and Animals Unlimited (www.birdsand animals.com) for twenty-five years. For eleven years, Mathilde worked with her dog Moose, who played Eddie on the television series *Frasier*. She worked with author Brian Hargrove to chronicle Moose's story in *My Life as a Dog*, Moose's autobiography.

Her movie credits include *Beginners*; *As Good as It Gets*; *Homeward Bound II*; *My Dog Skip*; *Lassie*; *A Dog Year*; *Marley & Me*; *Hotel for Dogs*; *Hugo*; *The Dictator*; *We Bought a Zoo*; and others. For more of Mathilde's credits, see www.imdb.com/name /nm0207692/. Interviews about and with Mathilde are available at http://focus features.com/video/cosmo_the_dog?film=beginners and www.traileraddict.com/trailer /beginners/interview-mathilde-decagny.

Claire Doré ("Bonny as the Shih Tzu in *Seven Psychopaths*: PAWSCAR Award Winner" and "Carrie Carrot and Harry as Tom Waits's Rabbit in *Seven Psychopaths*: A Constant Companion") attended Moorpark College's Exotic Animal Training and Management Program in 2000. She has worked as an animal trainer for over ten years and currently works for Performing Animal Troupe in Palmdale, California (www .performinganimaltroupe.com).

Claire has worked as an animal trainer on TV shows such as *The Closer* (trainer of Joel the cat); *Dexter*; *Criminal Minds*; *Rizzoli & Isles*; *Ray Donovan*; *True Jackson VP*; *iCarly*; *Rules of Engagement*; and *Greatest American Dog*. Her movie credits include *Seven Psychopaths*; *Marley & Me: The Puppy Years*; *Hot Tub Time Machine*; *Santa Buddies*; *The*

Resident; and *When a Stranger Calls*. You can find out more about Claire at www.imdb .com/name/nm1745610/. You can visit Bonny the shih tzu's Facebook page at www .facebook.com/BonnyShihTzu.

Thomas (Tom) Gunderson ("Crystal as the Capuchin in *Night at the Museum* and *We Bought a Zoo*: I *Am* a Monkey's Uncle") graduated from the Exotic Animal Training and Management Program at Moorpark College. He started his career with animals as an elephant keeper and trainer at the San Diego Wild Animal Park. Thomas is employed as an animal trainer in the film and television industry for Birds and Animals Unlimited. During his first twelve and a half years with the company, Thomas trained animals and performed at the Animal Actors Stage Show at Universal Studios Hollywood, where he was promoted to assistant manager.

Thomas has been caretaker and trainer of Crystal, a capuchin monkey, for more than seventeen years. He has worked with her on over ninety projects, including a starring role in the NBC comedy series *Animal Practice*. Thomas and Crystal have made appearances at numerous private functions in the media industry and have given educational presentations at schools in the Los Angeles area. Thomas's credits include the first two *Dr. Dolittle* movies; the first two *American Pie* films; the first two *Night at the Museum* features; *The Hangover Part II* and *Part III*; *Pirates of the Caribbean: On Stranger Tides*; *Indiana Jones and the Kingdom of the Crystal Skull*; *Transformers*; *The Dark Knight*; *Iron Man 2*; *Man of Steel*; *Cloverfield*; *Scream*; *A Dog Year*; *We Bought a Zoo*; *Zookeeper*; *Snow Dogs*; *Eight Below*; *3:10 to Yuma*; and *My Sister's Keeper*. To view more of Thomas's credits, see www.imdb.com/name/nm0348085/. You can view a short video of Thomas and Crystal on the set at www.youtube.com/watch?v=n7AvXEhbE48.

Thomas and his wife, Stacy, live with their two children, Logan and Jaden, in a rural area just outside Los Angeles, California. They run a nonprofit organization that operates a wildlife rescue facility and conducts entertaining educational programs.

Mark Harden ("Chico as Hachi in *Hachi: A Dog's Tale*: Forever Faithful," "Guido as Paulie in *Paulie*: The Sky's the Limit," and "Oscar as Butch in *Cats & Dogs: The Revenge of Kitty Galore*: The Right Dog for the Job") has been an animal-actor trainer for over thirty years. He is a senior trainer with Animals for Hollywood (www.boonesanimals .com) and has the uncommon ability to train multiple types of animal actors. He has been featured in Cesar Millan and Melissa Jo Peltier's book *Cesar's Rules: Your Way to Train a Well-Behaved Dog* and in articles in *Modern Dog* and *USA Today*.

His career as an animal trainer has taken him around the globe several times. He has trained a wide variety of animals who were principal characters in movies, including the seal in *The Golden Seal*; the chimp in *Project X*; the capuchin monkey in *Monkey Trouble*; the parrot Guido in *Paulie*; the cat Snowbell in *Stuart Little* and *Stuart Little 2*; the dog Butch in *Cats & Dogs* and *Cats & Dogs: The Revenge of Kitty Galore*; the Gambian rat Ben in *Willard*; and the Egyptian Mau Midnight in *Catwoman*.

Mark has been animal trainer, lead or head animal trainer, dog trainer or head dog trainer, or cat trainer for a long list of other popular movies and television series, including eight episodes of *True Blood*; *The Lone Ranger*; *Hachi: A Dog's Tale*; and three *Pirates of the Caribbean* movies. For more of Mark's credits, see www.imdb.com/name /nm0362103/. To see a demo reel of some animals Mark has trained, go to www.imdb .com/video/demo_reel/vi3046349849/.

Rusty Hendrickson ("Cimarron as Blackie, the Horse in *True Grit*: A Rugged Individual") began his career in films in Montana. He has worked in over seventy horse movies and has been called "the greatest horse wrangler in the world" by producers and directors. He has been head wrangler on seven of the ten highest-grossing horse movies of all time.

Rusty is a versatile horseman who also does stunts and acts in films. He was wrangler, horse wrangler, boss wrangler, head or lead horse wrangler, lead trainer, or stunt coordinator in *Django Unchained*; *True Grit*; *Jonah Hex*; *3:10 to Yuma*; *Dreamer*; *Seabiscuit*; *Secretariat*; *Ride with the Devil*; *The Patriot*; *The Horse Whisperer*; *Wyatt Earp*; *Dances with Wolves*; and other films.

For a list of Rusty's credits, see www.imdb.com/name/nm0376805/. To view Rusty talking about training horses and his Montana ranch, go to "Rusty's Roost" at http://vimeo.com/73242094.

Bobby Lovgren ("Finder as Joey in *War Horse*: A Director's Dream Actor") has been horse trainer, head horse trainer, wrangler, master head wrangler, or animal trainer on twenty-two movies, including *The Lone Ranger*; *Mirror Mirror*; *War Horse*; *Cowboys & Aliens*; *The Legend of Zorro*; *The Mask of Zorro*; *Racing Stripes*; and *Seabiscuit*.

Bobby refuses to work on any movie that does not have the American Humane Association level of safety standards for animal actors.

For more about Bobby and Finder, see www.imdb.com/name/nm0522463/ and www.facebook.com/FindersKey.

Larry Madrid ("Pinky and Richard Dent as the Penguins in *Mr. Popper's Penguins*: Keeping It Cool") started training animals in 1976 and worked at Magic Mountain, San Diego Zoo, and Universal Studios. Since 1992, he has trained animals for Birds and Animals Unlimited (www.birdsandanimals.com).

Larry has been animal trainer, head or lead animal trainer, or coordinator on *Forrest Gump*; *Batman Begins*; *Charlotte's Web*; *The Girl with the Dragon Tattoo*; *Mr. Popper's Penguins*; *Marley & Me*; *Harry Potter and the Sorcerer's Stone*; and other films. His work has been profiled in the *Wall Street Journal* and *Los Angeles Times*. For Larry's full credits, see www.imdb.com/name/nm0535108/.

Steve Martin ("Thunder, Harley, Shadow, and Cody as the Wolves of *True Blood*, *The Vampire Diaries*, *Teen Wolf*, and *Game of Thrones*: Walking on the Wild Side"), owner of Working Wildlife, has been one of the main suppliers and trainers of animal actors for over forty years. His company has over one hundred animal actors who have appeared in feature films, television series, commercials, videos, print ads, and other venues. From bottle-feeding to adulthood, Steve's trainers each care for and train the animals with whom they will work. They raise the animals in their homes with their families.

Working Wildlife has an education program in which a professional trainer takes animals to schools to teach children about them, and children come to the ranch for tours. See http://bit.ly/MDKNhq for a video clip of the program.

Working Wildlife has provided animals, and animal training, wrangling, and handling, for films and television series, including *True Blood*; *The Vampire Diaries*; *Game of Thrones*; *The Book of Eli*; *Spike*; *Resident Evil*; *Deadwood*; *Mrs. Santa Clause*; *The Three Stooges*; *And Man Created Dog*, distributed by the National Geographic Channel; and for commercials for Alpo, the American Cancer Society, Bud Light, Budweiser, Burger King, Coca-Cola, Disney, and Hallmark. For more information, go to www.working wildlife.com. You can see Steve on set with *True Blood*'s wolves at www.youtube.com /watch?v=yJzInUE_3Qo.

Rex Peterson ("Hightower in *The Horse Whisperer* and *Runaway Bride*: The Horse with an Actors' Equity Card") is credited as horse trainer or wrangler for over forty movies that span more than thirty years. His movie credits include *The Horse Whisperer*; *Black Beauty*; *Return of the Black Stallion*; *City Slickers*; *The Ring*; *Dracula*; *Hannah Montana: The Movie*; *Snow White*; *The Princess Diaries 2*; *All the Pretty Horses*; *Secretariat*; *Temple Grandin*; *Dreamer*; *Hidalgo*; *The Patriot*; *Arthur*; *Winter's Tale*; *The Knick*; and *The Lone Ranger*. More of Rex's credits can be found at www.swansonpetersonproductions.com /equine-film-stars and www.imdb.com/name/nmo677352/. You can see Rex training a horse at www.youtube.com/watch?v=holFimz2MKo. Rex delivers the shots required in a timely and safe manner and always has over a dozen highly trained horses ready for work.

Christina Potter ("Gable as Willie Nelson in *Our Idiot Brother*: From Agility Champion to Animal Actor") works with the All Star Animals and Animals for Advertising agencies in New York and has been an animal-actor trainer since 2000. She was the animal trainer for *Our Idiot Brother*, which featured her golden retrievers Gable, Kelly, and Hudson. You can see Christina's movie credits at www.imdb.com/name/nm2541094 and Gable's résumé at www.shermanarts.com/shermanarts/Gables_Resume.html.

Christina is the author of a novel about life as an animal actor, *Chester Gigolo: Diary of a Dog Star*. She currently works with her golden retriever (Hudson), a Chinese crested (Morgan), and a Berger Picard (Chester) on movie and commercial work (Verizon, *Project Runway*). Christina's website is www.shermanarts.com.

Karen Rosa ("Higgins as Benji, and Frank Inn, the Father of Humane Training: Inspiring a Million Shelter-Pet Adoptions") is senior adviser for the Film and Television Unit of American Humane Association (AHA). She has worked in executive positions for the organization since 1992. Karen was a producer of AHA's Amazing Animal Actors Tribute to Frank Inn and Benji presentation in 1998.

In her many positions over the years, primarily in the Film and Television Unit,

Karen has experienced the growth and professionalism of the program from a very hands-on perspective. Appreciating the magic and artistry that the exceptional trainers express through the animals they train, and with whom they bond, makes her work in this program both a passion and a joy.

Cari Swanson ("Hightower in *The Horse Whisperer* and *Runaway Bride*: The Horse with an Actors' Equity Card") grew up in Lexington, Ohio, in a family of equestrians, where she was around horses every day. She is friend and business partner to the renowned horse trainer Rex Peterson in their company, Swanson Peterson Productions at Windrock Farm in Millbrook, New York (www.swansonpetersonproductions.com).

Cari is a United States Dressage Federation silver medalist and is also involved with the Swedish Warmblood Breeding Program and the Rescue and Rehabilitation Program for injured horses. She works with Olympic riders and trainers, renowned judges, and great equestrians from around the world. Cari's equestrian expertise is sought after by top film and television producers and directors, such as Ang Lee and Steven Soderbergh. Her credits include *American General*; *Taking Woodstock*; *Arthur*; *The Knick*; *Winter's Tale*; and *Jayne Mansfield's Car*. She also provides horses for documentaries and television.

Jules Sylvester ("Kitty as the Burmese Python in *Snakes on a Plane*: How You Don't 'Train' Snakes and Insects") is a wildlife expert and animal trainer with an encyclopedic knowledge of animals, including amphibians, reptiles, and insects, all of which he supplies and wrangles through his company, Reptile Rentals, Inc. (www.reptile rentals.com).

His work has been featured by the Associated Press, PEOPLEPets.com, and the *Pittsburgh Post-Gazette*, among other media outlets. He regularly lectures in his entertaining style at universities and colleges and hosts Discovery Channel specials. In 2002, he had his own television series, *Wild Adventures*. Jules did the narration for Animal Kingdom at Disney World in Florida.

Jules has been a snake or animal wrangler and handler, actor, or stunt man for *CSI* (all the franchises); *The Tonight Show with Jay Leno*; *The Daily Show with Jon Stewart*; *Jimmy Kimmel Live*; *Desperate Housewives*; Spike TV's *1000 Ways to Die*; *Indiana Jones and the Kingdom of the Crystal Skull*; *Arachnophobia*; *Collateral Damage*; *Galaxy Quest*; *Casino Royale*; *Minority Report*; *Snakes on a Plane*; *Lemony Snicket's A Series of Unfortunate Events*; *Dr. Dolittle 2*; *The X-Files* TV series; *There's Something about Mary*; *Godzilla*; *Jurassic Park*; *The Lost World: Jurassic Park*; *Out of Africa*; and other productions. For more of Jules's credits, see www.imdb.com/name/nm0843230/.

Nicholas Toth ("Casey as Baloo the Bear in the *Jungle Book* Movies: Where's the Closest KFC?" and "Hollyberry as a Deer on *NCIS* and *The Mentalist*: The Indestructible Deer"), son of George Toth, grew up in the entertainment industry and has been a second-generation animal trainer for film, television, and commercials since 1964. He and his aunt Helena Walsh, wife, Kari Toth, and sister Elizabeth Chamberlain own and operate Cougar Hill Ranch in Palmdale, California, where they train and house animals. Some of these animals include those who cannot live in the wild and are brought to the ranch by the California Department of Fish and Wildlife.

Nicholas has trained and provided animals for a long list of movies, television series, and advertisements, including *Rudyard Kipling's The Jungle Book*; *The Jungle Book: Mowgli's Story*; *Back to the Future*; *Because of Winn-Dixie*; *Wolf*; *The Lion King*; *Reservoir Dogs*; *Evan Almighty*; *Dr. Dolittle* and *Dr. Dolittle 2*; *The New Swiss Family Robinson*; *It Came from Outer Space II*; and *Back to the Future Part III*. His work also includes commercials for Kodak, Purina ONE, and Lincoln-Mercury. He has provided animals for *The Tonight Show* since the 1970s. For more of Nicholas's credits, see www .imdb.com/name/nm0869353/.

Julie Tottman ("Crackerjack as Crookshanks, Hermione's Cat in the Harry Potter Films: Right Cat for the Job") is head animal trainer / coordinator for Birds and Animals UK. She was head animal trainer for *Harry Potter and the Half-Blood Prince*; *Harry Potter and the Order of the Phoenix*; *Harry Potter and the Goblet of Fire*; and *Harry Potter and the Sorcerer's Stone*; and animal trainer for *Harry Potter and the Chamber of Secrets*.

Julie has been a trainer or animal trainer, working with dogs, birds, and other animals, for a number of other productions, including *Sherlock Holmes*; *Resident Evil*; *Mamma Mia!*; *Bridget Jones*; and *Finding Neverland*. Julie was head puppy trainer for *102 Dalmatians*; dog trainer for *Lassie*; and trainer of birds and animals for *The Dark Knight*. She was animal wrangler for *The Woman in Black* and for eight episodes of *Game of Thrones*. For more of Julie's credits, see www.imdb.com/name/nm0869438/.

Omar von Muller ("Uggie as the Jack Russell Terrier in *The Artist*, and Jumpy: A Family of Dog Stars") grew up in an animal-loving family in Colombia, South America. For over thirty years, he has trained dogs, including his border collie–blue heeler mix Jumpy, for music videos, movies, and commercials. He is best known as trainer of Uggie, canine star of the Academy Award–winning movie *The Artist*, for which Omar was a head trainer. A highlight of Omar's and Uggie's careers was having Uggie be the first dog to have his paw prints on the Hollywood Walk of Fame (see www.zimbio.com /Omar+von+Muller).

Omar, Uggie, and Jumpy have been featured in national newspapers and maga-zines worldwide. Omar's television appearances with Uggie have included *The Today Show*, *Ellen*, and *Live with Regis and Kelly*. His credits include animal trainer in *Water for Elephants*, dog trainer in *Mr. Fix It*, and animal trainer in *What's Up, Scarlet?* For more on Omar, including movie credits and news stories, see www.imdb.com/name /nm1955301/.

Wendy Holden and Omar von Muller are the personal biographers for Uggie's memoir, *Uggie — My Story*. Omar's dog-training website is www.trainingwithomar.com.

PHOTOGRAPHER CREDITS

Except for the following, the photographs accompanying the stories in this book were taken by the contributors.

Foreword

Part 1

KEY TO JACKET PHOTOS

Richard Gere and puppy on set of *Hachi: A Dog's Tale* (see chapter 6)

Peanut flushing a toilet in *Meet the Fockers* (see chapter 19)

Finder and Bobby Lovgren (see chapter 1) © Ali Bannister

Bonny in director's chair (see chapter 9)

From left to right: Thunder, Harley, and Cody
(see chapter 10)

Crystal painting (see chapter 5)

Uggie (left) and Jumpy (right) (see chapter 11)

Frank Inn and Benji (Higgins) (see chapter 16)

Film Fauna's bobcat Ruby Rose with Casey Anderson on
Late Night with Conan O'Brien (see chapter 18)

Bonny on a bus bench with her movie poster
(see chapter 9)

Peanut and Robert De Niro (see chapter 19)

Chico at home (see chapter 6)

Hollyberry (see chapter 4)

Penguins in *Mr. Popper's Penguins* (see chapter 8)

Gidget on the set of *Legally Blonde 2: Red, White & Blonde* (see chapter 13) © Gayle Phelps and Sue Chipperton

American Humane Association certified animal safety representative Chris Obonsawin and Britney

ABOUT ROBIN GANZERT, PhD

Robin Ganzert, PhD, is president and CEO of American Humane Association, the first national humane organization, founded in 1877. Robin is a passionate advocate for the power of the child-animal bond. She is the mother of three children, and her family includes three dogs and two cats. She also loves movies and became a fan of animals in entertainment at a young age thanks to many Disney movies featuring beloved animal stars.

ABOUT
ALLEN AND LINDA ANDERSON

Allen and Linda Anderson are coauthors of a series of popular books, published in multiple languages, about the benefits of human-animal companionship. In 1996, they cofounded the Angel Animals Network to honor and expand upon their lifelong love of animals. Angel Animals uses the power of inspirational stories to increase love and respect for all life. The Andersons' books have won recognition from the American Society of Journalists and Authors Outstanding Book Award program. Allen and Linda were named Partners and Friends of American Humane Association in recognition that their mission and efforts are in alignment with the organization's work. The Andersons raised two children along with pets as family members. They currently share their home in Minneapolis with pets whose relationships would make great film plots — a dog named Leaf, Cuddles the cat, and Sunshine, a cockatiel who says, "I love you, sweet baby."

Angel Animals Network
PO Box 16682
Minneapolis, MN 55416
angelanimals@aol.com
www.angelanimals.net

ABOUT AMERICAN HUMANE ASSOCIATION

American Humane Association has, since 1877, been at the forefront of every major advancement in protecting children, pets, and farm animals from abuse and neglect. Today, American Humane Association is leading the way in understanding human-animal interaction and its role in society. The mission of American Humane Association is to ensure the welfare, wellness, and well-being of children and animals and to unleash the full potential of the bond between humans and animals to the mutual benefit of both.

National Headquarters:
American Humane Association
1400 16th St. NW, Suite 360
Washington, DC 20036
(800) 227-4645
info@americanhumane.org

Film and Television Office:
American Humane Association
Film and Television Unit
11530 Ventura Blvd.
Studio City, CA 91604
(818) 501-0123
filmunit@americanhumane.org

www.americanhumane.org

NEW WORLD LIBRARY is dedicated to publishing books and other media that inspire and challenge us to improve the quality of our lives and the world.

We are a socially and environmentally aware company. We recognize that we have an ethical responsibility to our customers, our staff members, and our planet.

We serve our customers by creating the finest publications possible on personal growth, creativity, spirituality, wellness, and other areas of emerging importance. We serve New World Library employees with generous benefits, significant profit sharing, and constant encouragement to pursue their most expansive dreams.

As a member of the Green Press Initiative, we print an increasing number of books with soy-based ink on 100 percent postconsumer-waste recycled paper. Also, we power our offices with solar energy and contribute to non-profit organizations working to make the world a better place for us all.

Our products are available in bookstores everywhere.

www.newworldlibrary.com

At NewWorldLibrary.com you can download our catalog,
subscribe to our e-newsletter, read our blog,
and link to authors' websites, videos, and podcasts.

Find us on Facebook, follow us on Twitter, and watch us on YouTube.

Send your questions and comments our way!
You make it possible for us to do what we love to do.

Phone: 415-884-2100 or 800-972-6657
Catalog requests: Ext. 10 | Orders: Ext. 52 | Fax: 415-884-2199
escort@newworldlibrary.com

NEW WORLD LIBRARY
publishing books that change lives   14 Pamaron Way, Novato, CA 94949

784